FINALLY

USING DIGITAL MEDIA

TO RESTORE CULTURE

AND BETTER OUR WORLD

HUMAN

BOB HUTCHINS

FINALLY HUMAN

Published by Franklin House Publishing, Franklin, Tennessee

FINALLY HUMAN

ENDORS EMENTS

THANK YOU

I would like to thank my wife, Kellie, for always believing and supporting me in everything I do. You demonstrate and live this book daily. My children, Riley, Lauren, and Sean. You are such an inspiration. Keep asking questions and never lose your wonder.

To Ben Richardson, I couldn't have completed this without you. Thank you so much for the hours you put into this.

Finally, the BuzzPlant team. What a great group of friends and colleagues. I am blessed to be able to live life with you all.

From start-ups to CEOs of established companies, there is something in *Finally Human* for everyone. It's nearly impossible to come up with timeless advice in the digital space but Bob Hutchins has done it here.
–Ash Greyson, Founder Ribbow Media

Finally Human rocks the way we see brand communications. Hutchins shows his readers how to take off the masks and create content and experiences that restore the humanity in all of us. Who thought 'marketing' could be this impactful?
–Joel Comm, New York Times Best-Selling Author

As someone who knows the importance of using digital media as it pertains to reaching an audience, what Bob has here is a book that truly bridges the gap between the digital world and human connection.
–Jarrid Wilson, Author and Blogger

I've had the privilege to be up close and personal with Bob for some time now and the thing most don't know is he lives and breathes what you'll read in *Finally Human*. This stuff isn't theory. It's not advice. It's the product of a lifetime of adventures in leading others (like me) in restoring culture and changing our world.
-Josh Collins, Digital Communications Manager, VisitFranklin.com

Bob Hutchins is a digital and social media expert. But he is also much more than this. In my experience, Bob is first and foremost a human being in relationship with other human beings. He runs his business like a family, engages his family with warmth and presence, serves his faith community with wisdom and commitment, engages his neighbors, and has many friends but no enemies. Bob is also a champion for health and flourishing, especially in relation to the digital world in which we live. He has taught, coached, and mentored organizations and individuals, myself included, in this path. The ideas in this book represent the sum of Bob's best insights. If you are looking for ways to optimize digital platforms without losing your integrity or your soul, *Finally Human* is the book for you. Enjoy!
–Scott Sauls, Senior Pastor of Christ Presbyterian Church in Nashville, Tennessee, and author of *Jesus Outside the Lines*

Bob's understanding of the current digital environment is spot-on! *Finally Human* breaks down the complex digital landscape and provides tactical steps for achieving inspired communities that any leader or organization will benefit from. Thoroughly enjoyed!
–Willie Morris, Founder and CEO of Faithbox

INTRO
DUCT
ION

WHAT IF
TECHNOLOGY
COULD INSPIRE
US TO BE
MORE HUMAN?

riticisms from every angle.

preventing us from creating "real" relationships.

Our iPhones cut us off from experiencing the world around us.

Our kids are growing up with "emotion atrophy."[1]

In short, technology – despite its benefits – is stifling our humanity and inhibiting our innate, never-before-interrupted ability to experience the world around us. At least, that's the story you'd hear if you paid attention to the average man on the street.

Does our contemporary digital environment have its problems? You bet. Researchers have created a term for the fear of being without your smartphone: nomophobia. And just how widespread *is* this addiction/fear? According to *Psychology Today*, nomophobia affects approximately **40 percent** of the population.[2]

It's a fair criticism that many of these "nomophobics," while connecting with a broader digital landscape, are shutting out their friends and family, and essentially depriving themselves of experiencing the immediate world within their range of perception. Smartphones, constant connectivity, social media usage, and the dull drone of incessant ping notifications can easily be labeled as sources of alienation.

Not only can the critics point to alienation. They would also be right to bring up the mean-spirited behaviors found on countless YouTube comment threads, internet forums, and teenage Snapchat Stories.

Of course, we haven't even talked about the big ones – **over-exposure** and **destruction of privacy**. "**30 percent** of all data transferred across the internet is porn," reports *The Huffington Post*.[3] If that's not troubling enough, consider that **one in ten** 12-13 year-olds are worried that they're *addicted* to porn. **One in five** had seen pornographic images, and "**12 percent** admitted to making or having been part of a sexually explicit video."[4]

Oh, and **privacy**? Not in today's world of data breaches[5], Snapchat leaks, and identity theft – all of which are made possible, or at least easier, through the technology found in the hand of every person you meet.

IS OUR TECHNOLOGY DESTROYING US?

It's a question folks have been asking since the invention of the Gutenberg Press. (Actually, Plato was concerned over 2,000 years ago that the technological advances of pen and paper would destroy one of the most basic and necessary human faculties: *memory*.[6]) The idea that new technology distances us from our own selves and each other is as old a thought as any.

When the telephone was invented, people were concerned that face-to-face interaction could die out. When email was popularized, we heard the cry of the death of handwritten letters. And Amazon should have wiped out all of the local grocery stores and retailers by now.

Despite these obvious challenges, what if this new, digital world isn't depriving us all of our humanity? What if technology is actually restoring, bit-by-bit, pieces of our humanity that were once lost? What if the elements of this digital landscape – wielded with proper reverence and emotional intelligence – could actually restore humanity back to the status it was meant to occupy?

THE DIGITAL ENVIRONMENT AS RESTORATIVE

As humans, we have an obligation to restore both the natural and artificial structures and environments that surround us. Those who work in *restorative* justice focus on meeting the needs of the perpetrators, victims and communities – as opposed to working for the satisfaction of what may be an outdated or irrelevant legal system. A restorative nurse's aide helps people regain strength and mobility. *Restoration* in the workplace is a beautiful thing because it's about so much more than a paycheck; it's about making the world a better place, as cliché-sounding as that may be.

How do those of us working in the digital landscape (which, these days, is just about everyone at some level) complete our work in a *restorative* manner? That's a question we're going to spend the rest of this book uncovering. Layer by layer, example by example, we'll discover together how technology and the vast array of digital communication tools available to us can be made *restorative*–and why that matters.

My friend and pastor, Scott Sauls, describes the role of a follower of Christ in this way: "We want to carry [Jesus's] grace, truth, and beauty into all of the places where we live, work, and play."[7]

Indeed, this desire to infuse the world with *grace, truth,* and *beauty* is one of the most natural feelings in the world. Here in Nashville, one of the country's fastest growing cities in the United States[8], there is a strong grassroots sentiment that the historical homes and irreplaceable relics of the music industry's early days are worthy of preservation. We have a community that views these properties (that a real estate developer might describe in dollar signs and decimal points) as structures with extraordinary intangible value. There's a frantic restorative spirit at work in the community, as people look to return neglected architectural relics to their former stature.

We see furniture built from "reclaimed" wood. Old scraps "repurposed" into beautiful jewelry. Vintage records "reimagined" in mashups and re-recordings. These are only small slivers, selective examples, of our very human desire to participate in restoration. We are all able to see an inherent value in the **people** who have come before us and the **things they have contributed** to the world. It's our natural inclination to preserve their work and their ways, while contributing to it the uniqueness that only *we* can bring.

Now, imagine what the world could look like if we could apply this deeply ingrained proclivity for restoration to our **digital environment**? What if the way we communicated through social media actually made another person more acutely aware of their own humanity? What if our email marketing – something typically perceived as incredibly sterile and *un*-human – actually *lifted* another person instead of annoyed them? Is it possible to sell a product and *genuinely* be your customer's friend? And most of all, are the critics right? Does our contemporary digital landscape fracture our humanity? Or can we actually leverage the technology and our new styles of communication to become more *fully human than we've ever been before?*

FINALLY HUMAN: ENRICHING OUR OWN HUMANITY & THE HUMANITY OF OTHERS

What if I told you that the technology you use and the way that you communicate could not only make *you* and *your brand* more human, but it could also enhance the humanity of those you relate with?

You don't have to be a non-profit. You don't need an emphasis in social-justice. You don't even have to be a business-to-consumer company. You just have to be *you*.

The problem is, we no longer know how to be ourselves. Communicating in our always-on digital world is hampered by constantly changing rules of netiquette, content saturation, and artificial distinctions between *brand* and *human* (to name a few of the problems).

It takes a lot to "just be you." One of my passions in digital restoration is to help individuals learn how to successfully and comfortably communicate in a way that adds value to their circles. In this book, we'll primarily cover digital/interactive communications, since this swiftly evolving space is where so many individuals and brands get trapped. However, the principles we'll look at carry over into all forms of communication.

WHO IS THIS BOOK FOR?

This book is for the listeners.

The talkers.

The screamers and the whisperers.

Whether you're the CMO of a Fortune 500 company or the founder of a brand new startup still working off a laptop in the kitchen... this book is for you. *Finally Human* tells the story of how brands communicate in a fast-growing digital culture where being "always-on" typically burns us out, turns us off, and shuts us down. In *Finally Human*, we will explore what it means to communicate (not *broadcast*) in a way that fills and energizes people.

WHAT WE'LL COVER IN FINALLY HUMAN

How Brands Thrive In the Age of Influence
Brands no longer control their image. If you've got nothing to hide, this

can still be a little intimidating. If you're not totally forthright and honest, this can be *terrifying*. We'll start things off by taking a deep dive into the Age of Influence, a label I apply to our current cultural atmosphere, where peer-recommendations and the ratings and reviews of complete strangers are perceived as more valuable and true than anything a brand can say for itself.[9] We will examine how brands are thriving in the Age of Influence and – more importantly – how the underlying philosophies that steer their marketing and communications can be adapted to *your* brand.

The most successful Age of Influence brands are ones that recognize and respond to people's natural, very human fears, desires, and hopes. Whether they appeal to the tenderness and insecurity of the heart, like Dove, or the carpe-diem thrill-seeker in us all, like Red Bull, these brands keep a finger on the cultural pulse, and know how to communicate in a way that enriches our lives.

100 Years of Brand Communications

Next, we'll take a few steps back to look at how brands have communicated in the past. There's a rich cultural, sociological, philosophical, economical, psychological history behind the last 100 years of communications. And, no, you don't have to be a communications geek to appreciate it. You only have to share an appreciation for *people*. The reason *why* is simple. Behind every company, there is a person; and behind every "target customer demographic," there is an individual.

Really, there is no such thing as business-to-business or business-to-consumer communications. All communication, when boiled down to its essence, is human-to-human. Of course, things didn't start out that way, which is why we'll be evaluating the communication shifts that have taken place over the last 100 years. This is a *fascinating* story – and one that you haven't heard before.

Four Pillars of The Age of Influence

For some communicators, fostering the *humanity* of your brand will beeasy; it just comes naturally. For most of us, that's not the case. As I said earlier, it takes a lot to "just be you."

Many of us had the impulse for natural, transparent speech driven out of us upon entering the professional world. We're told that it's good to be fast-responders, but company policies and clunky approval systems actually steer us *away* from brand-responsiveness. We know we should create relationships with our audiences that are built on trust, but we don't know what those *actually* look like in concrete, day-to-day terms.

And, of course, there's the big one: "authenticity." How can we show ourselves without revealing too much?

In this section of the book, we will explore what it means to be genuine, transparent, responsive, and trusted by consumers in The Age of Influence. We'll talk about how these notions have changed over the years, and why these pillars are so vital for thriving in today's digital environment.

Real Brands Enriching Our Humanity

Lastly, we'll pull down from the 30,000-foot view to talk brass tacks. I want *you* to have a rich understanding of what it means to communicate in a way that enhances the humanity of your brand and your audience. Imagine a world... or a Facebook feed... where business communications as we know them have been replaced by messages that don't bounce off of us, but resonate deep inside because they speak to a part of ourselves we ordinarily reserve for friends, family, or ourselves – if we're willing to open up at all. At the end of *Finally Human*, we'll look at three brands that are successfully communicating on this deeper, personal level.

WHY FINALLY HUMAN?

Lastly, I don't mean to give the impression through *Finally Human* that we are currently "less than human," and that technology is our redemption – far from it! Considering the totality and complexity of our humanity is beyond the scope of this book. As I said earlier, my personal *restorative* role is to ask questions about (a) what it means to become fully human and (b) what it means to enrich the humanity of others through brand communications. every part of our lives. Now, let's make them *meaningful* and *enriching*.

Most importantly, let me also state that "brand communications" is one very narrow silo in all of human communications. There are countless conversations and communication styles beyond this small subset, many of which are equally or more important to you, the reader, and myself. Matters of faith, personal relationships, wisdom, and legacy outweigh the significance of brand communications on any given day. There are plenty of brilliant authors who have discoursed on these ideas; none, however, have addressed the deeper implications of **marketing** and **advertising** on the human spirit. Up until the last few years, these two words (and all of the preconceptions tied to them) have been held in much lower regard than other aspects of our humanity. But when you consider their titanic roles in everyday life – whether we invite them or not – marketing and advertising are equally worthy of our critical evaluation. These forces have broken into every part of our lives. Now, let's make them *meaningful* and *enriching*.

In no way do I want to mislead anyone into thinking that marketing-in-the-digital-world is some great answer to a sense of despair, emptiness, or lost humanity. Rather, my aim with *Finally Human* is to focus on life-giving, meaningful behavior in one sliver of the world: the digital culture.

So, with those disclaimers out on the table, I invite you to join me in exploring all of the many potentials of personal and genuine communication. Let's start contributing to our digital culture in a way that enhances the humanity of those around us. Are you ready?

THE CHALLENGES OF TECHNOLOGY

The human condition is characterized by a state of brokenness. That statement probably isn't the inspiring lead-off you're looking for, but it's a true one. We are broken. As individuals, as families, as a culture, a state, a species. We get sick, we go to war, we disrespect one another. We're selfish, we're manipulative, we're frightened.

This innate brokenness largely characterizes who we are and what we do. We are all looking to escape the brokenness through whatever means and methods present themselves: dieting, yoga, religion, drugs, work, relationships, achievement, sex, hobbies, and money... every one of us could write a list that spills down the page and keeps going, and going, and going until it fills a book.

Brokenness affects us all; and we all have our own ways of dealing with it. Of course, technology is one of the easiest scapegoats we can point our fingers at. We *love* having a scapegoat, and the prevalence of all these personal devices, the constant connectivity, and the totally new ways of experiencing the world is all too easy to call out.

Besides, the evidence of technology's destructiveness is floating right there on the surface. We see our kids (and, let's be honest, *ourselves*) glued to the iPhone. We hold a nostalgia for the idyllic image of uninterrupted summer picnics and warm winter nights by a fire — those simple, quiet moments of quality family time.

But we don't do *quaint*. We do gigabit internet, live-Tweeting, and apps that tell us how many steps we take, how many friends we have, and everything in between. And for those reasons... we've come to resent ourselves. We describe technology as having a hold on our lives. It prevents us from enjoying our vacations and focusing on the friend across the table that is speaking to us. So, naturally, we blame *technology*. "Technology is the cause of my brokenness," we say to ourselves. "It's all of these apps, devices, listicles, emails, and people vying for my attention."

In a last-ditch effort to "fix" ourselves, we boldly proclaim, "I'm deleting my Facebook!" We read blog posts about how to get our email inbox to zero. We download internet-blocking apps, and try to convince ourselves that we'll be happier with a hobby than a Netflix subscription. At one point or another, we've all presented ourselves as mini-pseudo-Luddites.

And then we have to go back to work.

We have to get *this* app to keep in touch with our siblings, and *that* device to save on our utility bills, and *this* new computer to be able to run *that* new program, and on, and on, and on...

It's exhausting.

We run in constant circles: needing our technology, resenting it, swearing it off, and then finding ourselves forced to return to it. In order to actively and meaningfully participate in the world – at work, at home, and with friends – we have to use the technology. As this cycle has intensified and become even more demanding over the last two decades, we are getting increasingly frustrated.

WHERE DO WE GO FROM HERE?

This book isn't out to vilify technology. On the contrary, I'm going to show you the beautiful, restorative aspects of technology. However, in order to get to the beauty, we have to break through the ugly surface and address some of the gritty realities of technology's darker side. In this chapter, we're going to take a candid look at the challenges technology presents. I've narrowed these issues down to four broad topics: **Alienation, Addiction, Over-Exposure,** and **Loss of Privacy.**

These four challenges are nothing new; they are problems that have existed long before mass media and the web. However, they have now become **bigger** and more **prevalent** issues today than ever before. Sadly, these issues are creating a rift between us and all of the wonderful possibilities that dwell within our digital environment. In other words, if we can understand and address these Big Four issues, then we can learn to move past them and start exploring how technology can *enhance* – not *deprive us* of – our humanity. First, we must come to grips with the problems and develop empathy for those (including ourselves) who are affected.

As I said in the introduction, technology isn't our redemption, but it also doesn't have to be the disparaged source of our brokenness. Rather, the tools of technology can and *should* be **leveraged for restoration.** But first, the challenges...

ALIENATION: TECHNOLOGY AS A CURTAIN
BETWEEN US & THE WORLD

Sherry Turkle is a professor at MIT and the author of numerous books that explore the relationships between social media, technology, culture, and psychology. Turkle asks tough questions about how we use technology to relate (... or *disengage*) with one another. In 2012, she shared a TED talk, "Connected, but alone?"[10] that thoughtfully presents this paradoxical love-hate relationship technology forces upon us.

In her TED talk, Turkle makes the observation that technology isn't just a growing presence in our lives; it's actually *changing our relationships with others and ourselves.*

"People want to customize their lives," she says. "They want to go in and out of all the places they are because the thing that matters most to them is control over where they put their attention. So you want to go to that board meeting, but you only want to pay attention to the bits that interest you. And some people think that's a good thing. But you can end up hiding from each other, even as we're all constantly connected to each other."

This ability to drop in and drop out of the physical and digital spaces we are either (1) forced to inhabit or (2) occupy by choice subverts the fundamental realities of what it has meant to be a human being throughout our species' existence. We now have the dangerously unique ability to *choose* where we spend our time in the digital world. Our choices can lead to meaningful connections with others, or they can totally alienate us from healthy relationships.

"Technology appeals to us most where we are most vulnerable," says Turkle. "And we are vulnerable. We're lonely, but we're afraid of intimacy. And so from social networks to sociable robots, we're designing technologies that will give us the illusion of companionship without the demands of friendship. We turn to technology to help us feel connected in ways we can comfortably control. But we're not so comfortable. We are not so much in control."

In recent years, these themes of connection, loneliness, and the need for control have suddenly appeared in every field, from news outlets, religious leaders and pop psychologists to film, comedy, and art. Perhaps one of the most viral examples of technology-is-alienating-us outrage comes from

comedian Louis C.K. on Conan. In this brief segment[11], Louis
into why he refuses to buy his kids cellphones:

"The thing is," he says, "you need to build an ability to just be y   n and
not be doing something. That's what the phones are taking away – is the
ability to just sit there like this. That's being a person, right? [...] You know,
underneath everything in your life there's that thing, that empty, forever
empty... you know what I'm talking about? [...] Sometimes when things clear
away, you're in your car and you go, oh, no, here it comes that I'm alone."

For Louis C.K., *that's* the moment where we turn to our phones. *That's*
the moment where we either look to connect with others or, more often
than not, simply distract ourselves with *anything* that can fill the void we
experience in that moment. Whether you share in his tongue-in-cheek
nihilism or find existence ripe with meaning, I think you would agree that
this sudden, acute sense of loneliness or despair is very real. I would also
presuppose that on more than a few occasions we've all sought some kind
of escape from those moments through our devices and social networks.

The 2013 Spike Jonze film *Her* pushes this theme of technology-as-
alienation to its inevitable and troubling dystopian conclusions. In the
movie, Theodore (played by Joaquin Phoenix) begins dating Samantha,
an OS (operating system, played by Scarlett Johansson) that exhibits
an extraordinary amount of artificial intelligence. Theodore initiates
the relationship at a vulnerable and lonely time in his life: after his wife
announces her intent to divorce. While the A.I. technology is considered
perfectly normal in the film's slightly futuristic Los Angeles setting,
Theodore is one of the first of many people to develop an abnormally
intimate relationship with his device.

Over the course of the film, Theodore and Samantha progressively adapt
to different levels of intimacy and (in Theodore's case) dependency. While
Theodore initially finds himself reconnecting with the world through his
relationship with Samantha, things take a turn for the worse, leaving him
as alienated as we found him at the beginning of the film. *Her* presents, in
a creative and fresh style, the now-common argument that our technology
draws us away from the "real" world. We see ourselves, all too painfully, in
Theodore.

Needless to say, technology doesn't have to be alienating. There is
hope yet. In the coming pages of this book, we're going to discuss real

FOR ALL ITS

BENEFITS,

TECHNOLOGY

HAS THE

CAPACITY

TO STUNT

THE **GROWTH**

OF OUR

EMOTIONAL

AND **SOCIAL**

INTELLIGENCES.

strategies for communicating in a way that draws people in and fills them in real, meaningful ways. Sherry Turkle offers this optimistic conclusion in her TED talk:

"Now we all need to focus on the many, many ways technology can lead us back to our real lives, our own bodies, our own communities, our own politics, our own planet. They need us. Let's talk about how we can use digital technology, the technology of our dreams, to make this life the life we can love."

DEVICE ADDICTION & DEPENDENCY

In addition to addressing alienation, *Her* is a strikingly apt commentary on the nature of dependency and addiction. The film's dependency-theory isn't just a scriptwriter's personal opinion. Sociologists and behavioral psychologists around the globe are finding cellphone addiction to be a significant problem in *all* demographics.

In 2015, researchers at the University of Missouri "[...] found that cell phone separation can have serious psychological and physiological effects on iPhone users, including poor performance on cognitive tests."[12]

One year earlier, in 2014, Baylor researcher Jim Roberts, Ph.D., published the results of a study on cellphone addiction in male and female college students.[13] His findings included these not-so-surprising figures:

• Some functions — among them Pinterest and Instagram — are associated significantly with cellphone addiction.

• But others that might logically seem to be addictive – Internet use and gaming — were not.

• Women college students spend 10 hours daily on their cellphones. Men spend nearly 8 hours per day on their phones.

It is no wonder that we find it hard to concentrate – difficult to go several hours without our devices feeding us information, entertainment, distractions, and the promise of social belonging.

OVER-EXPOSED, OVER-STIMULATED & OVERWHELMED

Sadly, addiction to our devices and social networks isn't the only form of addiction that our technology has stimulated. Internet pornography is the elephant in the room when it comes to web-related addiction.

Pornography accounts for a shocking **30 percent** of all data transferred across the internet.[14] Studies suggest that the adult entertainment industry generates $13 billion of revenue per year, reaches 90% of boys and 60% of girls before the age of 18, and makes its first impression on children at the age of 11 (median age).[15] Its use is on the rise, affecting more people today than ever before.[16]

Porn consumption isn't an exclusively male issue. According to a report from the Pew Research Center, online porn viewership amongst women quadrupled between 2010 and 2013.[17]

But pornography is an easy target. We *know* that pornography is attacking our families at every opportunity. It's slightly more difficult to see the other ways in which we are over-exposed, over-stimulated, and – ultimately – overwhelmed by our digital environment.

Phillip Zimbardo, psychologist at Stanford University, has extensively explored the effects of all this over-stimulation on boys, specifically, in *Man (Dis)Connected: How Technology Has Sabotaged What it Means to be Male*, co-authored with Nikita D. Coulombe. The book draws on data from 20,000 young men to establish a correlation between a "masculinity crisis" and excessive video game and pornography use.

In a Ted Talk[18], four years before the publication of *Man (Dis)Connected*, Zimbardo presents compelling data for the case that boys are falling behind girls in academics and social behavior (higher dropout rate, lower college graduation rates, increased likelihood of ADD, etc.). Zimbardo blames these problems on the overstimulation provided to boys by excessive video gameplay and pornography use – two activities that typically occur in an isolated environment, where boys are able to be in control and get what they want.

"The problem is they now prefer [the] asynchronistic Internet world to the spontaneous interaction in social relationships," says Zimbardo. "What are the causes? [...] I think it's excessive Internet use in general, excessive video

gaming, excessive new access to pornography. The problem is these are arousal addictions. [...] And the problem is the industry is supplying it. Jane McGonigal told us last year that by the time a boy is 21, he's played 10,000 hours of video games, most of that in isolation."

In concluding his Ted Talk, Zimbardo suggests, "Boys' brains are being digitally rewired in a totally new way for change, novelty, excitement and constant arousal. That means they're totally out of sync in traditional classes, which are analog, static, interactively passive. They're also totally out of sync in romantic relationships, which build gradually and subtly."

In other words, our technology – and the opportunities it creates for us – is developing faster than we are. We suddenly have access to more content than we know what to do with. For readers in my generation, we can remember back to the time when the world was different – when information was limited, social interaction required stepping out into the world (or at least picking up the phone), and sometimes you just had to be bored.

Late Millennials/"Generation Z" have never had to face any of these same challenges. Instead, this newest generation performs better in the artificial world than the "real" one. This is an issue that keeps PhD and author Jane McGonigal (referenced above) up at night. McGonigal is the author of *Reality is Broken: Why Games Make Us Better and How They Can Change the World*. She is frequently included on lists of the world's most creative, inspiring, and humanitarian business people.

McGonigal describes the root of her problem in a Ted Talk[19] as follows: "When we're in game worlds, I believe that many of us become the best version of ourselves – the most likely to help at a moment's notice, the most likely to stick with a problem as long at it takes, to get up after failure and try again. And in real life, when we face failure, when we confront obstacles, we often don't feel that way. We feel overcome, we feel overwhelmed, we feel anxious, maybe depressed, frustrated or cynical. We never have those feelings when we're playing games, they just don't exist in games."

Our video games – our artificial realities – provide us with the stimulation we *want*, the challenges we can *overcome*, and the option to walk out at any time. For a generation that grows up spending 10,000 hours in front of a video game console by the age of 21, reality is a harsh wake-up call. (McGonigal does present an innovative way of turning this problem into a solution. I recommend watching her Ted Talk to learn more.)

Suffice it to say, for all its benefits, technology has the capacity to stunt the growth of our emotional and social intelligences.

OUR LIVES ARE PUBLIC... WHETHER WE LIKE IT OR NOT

In June 2013, Edward Snowden, a former system administrator for the CIA and contractor with the National Security Agency (NSA), leaked thousands of classified documents, revealing the existence of several top-secret mass surveillance programs that monitor ordinary U.S. citizens. Snowden's leaks informed us:[20]

- The U.S. government collects nearly all Americans' phone records and 200 million text messages per day.

- The NSA can, by law, request user data from major servers (Google, Facebook, etc.).

- The XKeyScore can track a web user's every move online.

- The NSA attempted to "infiltrate links connecting Yahoo and Google data centers, behind the companies' backs."

And that's just the beginning. The American public is waking up to the Post-Snowden Era, where privacy is a concept that's quickly fracturing under the weight of Big Data. August and September 2014's Apple iCloud leaks, which included nude images of hundreds of celebrities, further weakened Americans' sense of privacy and security.

In November 2014, the Pew Research Center shared the American public's sentiments with regards to online privacy and security: [21]

- 91% of adults in the survey "agree" or "strongly agree" that consumers have lost control over how personal information is collected and used by companies.

- 88% of adults "agree" or "strongly agree" that it would be very difficult to remove inaccurate information about them online.

- 80% of those who use social networking sites say they are concerned about third parties like advertisers or businesses accessing the data they share on these sites.

Faith in social media, email, and instant message security is dropping. According to the same report, "81% feel 'not very' or 'not at all secure' using social media sites when they want to share private information with another trusted person or organization. 68% feel insecure using chat or instant messages to share private information. 58% feel insecure sending private info via text messages."

As public opinion on privacy and security shifted, it's no wonder that Google shut the lid on its controversial Google Glass project just a few months later in February 2015.[22]

Our lives are no longer private. It's been a painful realization for many teens applying to college and young adults interviewing for their first job. In *It's Complicated: The Social Lives of Networked Teens*, author Danah Boyd talks about some of the privacy and contextual challenges experienced by the teens she came across in researching for her book. In one chapter, she shares the story of a teenage boy from South Central Los Angeles, who wrote a brilliant Ivy League application essay.[23] But while his essay contained hopes and aspirations to leave behind the neighborhood gangs, his MySpace page told a very different story, showing reference after reference to gang activity.

Boyd's theory is that the teenager used his MySpace page for protection. Without it, he could become a victim of the gang. He may have perceived his MySpace page as his only opportunity to survive and escape. The thought had not occurred to him that the same MySpace page that keeps him alive in Los Angeles could crush any hopes for a better future after high school.

Boyd's example is a good reminder that privacy is multifaceted and platforms serve different purposes. First, we require a very basic, fundamental privacy – one that protects us from governments, corporations, and the public. Second, we desire the privacy to be able to share certain things on Instagram, which won't be seen by employers, but will be visible to our friends, but private from our family, et cetera, et cetera. Many of us have been guilty of the naïve expectation that we can appear *one* way on Web Platform A and *another* way on Web Platform B.

Of course, that's just not the case. Our privacy is shrinking, but we have the power to control our response to this new reality.

EMPATHY *and* UNDERSTANDING

should be the

NATURAL STARTING POINT

for ANYONE

who wants to

TRULY UNDERSTAND

what it means to

COMMUNICATE

in a way that

ENRICHES *and* FULFILLS

AN AUDIENCE.

EMPATHY: THE STARTING POINT IN COMMUNICATION

Is the state of our digital culture really so dismal? Are we really all so lonely, alienated, over-stimulated, and exposed to an endless stream of privacy vulnerabilities? I would argue not. While the problems detailed in this chapter are very real, they aren't the ending to our story.

As people who *care* about our audiences, their needs, and their communication styles, we have to learn their struggles (and our own) in order to communicate honestly and meaningfully. We must first understand why the mom of middle-school children is worried about all of the social networks her children's friends are signing up for. We have to put ourselves in the shoes of the workaholic who spends 16 hours a day in front of a laptop screen or on her phone. We need to identify with the lonely 30-something who finds his work isolating and his iPhone an extension of his alienating circumstances.

As Stephen Covey, author of *The 7 Habits of Highly Effective People*, says, "When you show deep empathy toward others, their defensive energy goes down, and positive energy replaces it. That's when you can get more creative in solving problems."[24]

Empathy and understanding should be the natural starting point for anyone who wants to *truly* understand what it means to communicate in a way that enriches and fulfills an audience. In the next chapter, we'll take a hyper-speed tour through one hundred years of brand communications (Part B of our "empathy tour"). Then, in chapter three, we'll dive into how we can begin the process of restoring our digital environment.

HOW DID WE GET HERE? 100 YEARS OF BRAND COMMUNICATIONS

To say advertising has changed over the last 100 years is an understatement. Not only have the tools of the trade been completely redeveloped, but the objectives, styles, and content of today's brand communications have come so far they would be virtually *unrecognizable* to someone in the business back in 1915.

There are the obvious technological developments, of course. But just as significant are the changes in *how* brands communicate. Instead of churning out a constant stream of BUY-OUR-STUFF messaging, brands have started to increase their focus on *story*.

While it would be nice to think that this shift toward *story* is the natural result of some collective goodwill discovered by advertisers worldwide... I'm more inclined to think the shift was *forced* upon brands.

Let's face it: these last few decades, we've all become somewhat jaded toward advertising.

Not only have we been constantly bombarded with consumer-oriented messaging... but the *times* and *places* where these messages have been able to reach us have grown exponentially.

We've been sold to at every possible time and place an advertiser could weasel their way into. Take your eyes up from this book, and I bet you can find at least one advertisement around you. Whether you're on the L-Train in Brooklyn, a beach in Cabo, or your living room couch... you are almost *guaranteed* to be the object of some pesky, intruding advertiser.

We're sick of it. And advertisers know it. So, what do they do? They turn to that human element that resonates with *everyone*: **story.**

WHAT YOU NEED TO KNOW
ABOUT WOMEN-WHO-WEAR-SNEAKERS

Women-Who-Wear-Sneakers don't care about a full-page ad with a picture of your latest shoe. There are a million full-page ads. There are a million shoes. What do you have to offer *that woman?*

But Women-Who-Wear-Sneakers-and-Care-About-Social-Justice *are* interested in a documentary that reveals the exploitive conditions of overseas shoe manufacturing. Oh, and that documentary? It was produced and screened by *your* sneaker company, which uses local materials and pays craftspeople a fair wage for their work. So, when you screen your new documentary in your retail space, suddenly you've created a **story-based connection** between your brand and your consumers.

What changed between the two scenarios (the full-page ad v. the documentary)? First, you decided to tell a story that is meaningful to your audience. And, secondly, you narrowed the definition of your audience by deciding that Women-Who-Wear-Sneakers is too broad. There's just too many of them, and they all have many different interests, income levels, and fashion styles. Instead, you decided to tell a story to a smaller niche audience: Women-Who-Wear-Sneakers-and-Care-About-Social-Justice. You don't have to spend the time *convincing* this audience that they should care about how their sneakers are made. They already agree with you. What they *didn't know* before seeing your documentary, however, was the truth of the mass-market shoe industry. Before they stepped into your retail space, they *didn't know* that your brand stands in direct opposition to the economically repressive and socially unjust practices of mass-market shoe production.

You told a story. To a specific audience that *cares*.

But the world didn't always work this way. So, where did we come from, and how did we get to this point? My version of the story is loosely built on the framework established by journalist Kirsty Sharman.[25] In the following pages, we'll look at how brand communications – specifically in the light of *storytelling* – has changed over the last 100+ years.

WORD OF MOUTH ADVERTISING

Did you know that the first telephones were sold in pairs? When Alexander Graham Bell released his invention in 1876, buyers had to purchase *two* – one for each end of the conversation. Then, the buyer had to bring out a contractor to lay the line between the two telephones. If you wanted to talk to someone else, you had to buy another pair of telephones, and have your contractor come out again to lay an additional line.

In 1894, the switchboard was invented, finally making the use of telephones more practical for the mainstream. Still, it would take 50 years for Bell's invention to reach half of the U.S. population, and 80 years until nearly *everyone* had access to a telephone.[26]

The telephone was one of the first modern tools – second only to the telegraph – that significantly extended our ability to connect with others. With the advent of the telephone, households could communicate with each other more quickly and directly than ever before.

Very slowly, barriers to information would begin to crumble. With the telephone, consumers were given the ability to connect with each other in real time without the delay of written letters or the challenges of geographic isolation (which was very significant for early 20th century America's predominantly agrarian/rural society).

One ring at a time, the telephone was cracking open the door to unmonitored and uncontrolled consumer-to-consumer interaction. But, let's not get ahead of ourselves. While the telephone opened up some level of transparency and consumer awareness, it was no Yelp. Advertising content – you know, the slick, downright dishonest magazine ads you think of when you hear the words "*advertising content*" – was just getting started...

1920S: EDITORIAL & ADVERTORIAL

The "Roaring '20s" ushered in the first age of consumerism. As annual earnings increased and the traditional workweek scaled back from six to five days a week, the American middle-class found themselves with more money and more time.

Advertisers were more than happy to help them spend it – primarily by playing into fears and insecurities:

"Most men ask 'Is she pretty?' not 'Is she clever?'" (Palmolive)

"How's your breath today? If it's bad, you won't be welcome." (Listerine)

"Wash away fat and years of age." (La-Mar Reducing Soap)

This early age of advertising did an excellent job of casting visions of grandeur for consumers. (And also making them feel ashamed if they didn't buy the product.) Advertising became less about the product's features and more about developing a hungry consumer mindset. As Blackford and Kerr write in *Business Enterprise in American History*, "Before 1910, advertisers mostly sought to inform customers about products; after 1910, the main goal was to create a desire to purchase products."[27]

As scientific breakthroughs began to boom in the early part of the 20th century, many companies were quick to introduce new products full of promise to the marketplace. The changing face of the workweek and new expendable income only bolstered consumerism and the rise of the advertising industry.

"In 1919 advertising costs were 8 percent of total distribution costs in industry; by 1929, the share was 14 percent [nearly $3 billion]," write Blackford and Kerr.[28]

America was starting to change.

1920S-1930S: THE CONTENT/AD SPACE LOOP

During the 1920s (and then especially in the 1930s), radio established itself as one of the premier spaces for advertisers. At first, radio was the hobbyist's plaything. With the development of the Radiola by American Marconi (later known as RCA), radio entered into the mainstream. Still, the media didn't bear any resemblance to "radio" as *we* consider it. Early 1920s radio broadcasting was fully in the hands of amateur enthusiasts, who would borrow phonographs from friends or the nearby music store and spin them on air.

Soon, the novelty wore off; listeners wanted *more*. They longed for a *more* diverse music library; different voices; new types of information. But where would broadcasters find the funds?

Advertisers.

As AdAge Encyclopedia notes, "Commercial radio broadcasting found its foothold as a form of entertainment in the U.S. through a combination of factors, including economic depression, the influence of corporations,

Mass Appeal

ISN'T ALWAYS

ATTRACTIVE.

PEOPLE ARE

DIFFERENT.

THERE'S NO

SUCH THING

AS A "MASS"

PERSON.

urbanization, electrification and the recognition of production, consumption and distribution."[29]

While the adoption of radio happened relatively fast (1 in 500 households owned a receiver in 1921, and 1 in 6 households by 1926), the financial strategy moved more slowly for broadcasters. By 1927, only one in five radio programs had sponsors.[30]

Enter Big Tobacco and Big Agencies.

At the close of the 1920s, Camel, Lucky Strike and Chesterfield were battling it out on the radios, spending millions in advertising dollars. Agencies like L&T, JWT, Young & Rubicam, and BBDO were created to sell radio space.

More advertising dollars allowed for more content. More content meant more listeners. And more listeners meant more advertising.

A cycle was born.

1940S-1970S: MASS BROADCASTING

There was just one problem. Everyone was a part of the cycle. Advertisers were using mass marketing tools like print, radio, and television to speak to a *mass* audience. There was no distinction between demographic markets.

Remember Women-Who-Wear-Sneakers-and-Care-About-Social-Justice? Advertisers had not yet arrived at that niche mentality. Instead of creating stories that speak to a small, committed, ready-to-buy audience, advertisers were speaking to the masses. So, naturally, their stories had to have *mass appeal*.

But mass appeal isn't always attractive. People are different. There's no such thing as a "mass" person.

Mass marketing inevitably misses the mark with *individuals*, and its scattershot approach is expensive. Remember, this mass-broadcasting era predates the use of Big Data (for narrowing demographics) and personal devices/internet (for precision marketing). Advertisers were doing the best they could with what they had to start telling stories.

While many advertisements in this era continued to employ shame, guilt, and societal pressure to drive the consumerist mindset, there are many examples of advertisements from mid-20th century America that begin to tell a *story*.

Bob Levenson's "Snow Plow" ad for Volkswagen[31] is one of many such Volkswagen examples. "Have you ever wondered how the man who drives the snow plow drives to the snow plow?" asks the TV commercial's earnest narrator. "This one drives a Volkswagen," announces the voiceover, while showing the dark, frigid plight of the driver rumbling through piles of snow. Other classic Levenson/Volkswagen ads include "Think Small" and "Lemon," two iconic ads featuring the VW Beetle. Concerning the Lemon ad, which pairs a picture of the vehicle with the headline "Lemon." and three small columns of copy, Levenson had this to say:

"It was a pretty audacious thing for a car company to call its own car a lemon. It's still audacious to run a picture of your product with a headline suggesting something is wrong with it. But it was such an arresting combination, and when you read the ad, you found out the car was a lemon because it had a scratch on the glove compartment and was rejected just because of that. The last line was, 'We pluck the lemons, and you get the plums.' "[32]

Volkswagen told a *story*.

It's no wonder that American ad exec Jerry Della Femina says, "In the beginning, there was Volkswagen. That was the day when the new advertising agency was really born."[33]

With ad agencies like DDB (for whom Levenson wrote the Volkswagen ads), advertising took a few long strides into a totally new frontier. The environment was still characterized by "mass-to-mass" communication, but *story* and *art* had begun to emerge.

1980S-2000S: AD-AS-PRODUCT, STORYTELLING & TARGETED MESSAGING

Video killed the radio star... and MTV presided over the entire funeral by introducing a new way of perceiving the relationship between product, advertisement, and seller. In the past, advertisers *sponsored* content. On MTV, which launched in 1981, the advertisement *was* the content. Even more remarkable, MTV found a way to get consumers to willingly tune into the content.

Viewers tuned in to watch their favorite bands and artists, which resulted in their exposure to more bands and artists. The music industry – which was not producing many music videos at this time – saw an opportunity for promotion, and quickly began creating more music videos, which would air on MTV, thereby increasing the value of the channel for both viewers and content producers.

The value of the video isn't limited to those in the music industry. Product placement quickly became a monetization strategy for many consumer goods. From cars to alcohol, brand names of all types began cropping up in the music videos that MTV aired to millions around the world.

(By 2009, product placement in music videos had become a $3.6 billion industry.[34]) Everything from Miracle Whip to Mini Coopers had a supporting role in music videos.

The advertising-as-product model has dramatically shifted how today's businesses think about advertising. As marketing guru Seth Godin has written, "The secret of big-time advertising during the 1960s and '70s was the "big idea." In *A Big Life in Advertising*, ad legend Mary Wells Lawrence writes, "'... our goal was to have big, breakthrough ideas, not just to do good advertising. I wanted to create miracles.' A big idea could build a brand, a career, or an entire agency."[35]

This is the *old* way: the way that doesn't necessarily work post-MTV. As Godin suggests, "Today, the advertiser's big idea doesn't travel very well. Instead, the idea must be embedded into the experience of the product itself. Once again, what we used to think of as advertising or marketing is pushed deeper into the organization. Let the brilliant ad guys hang out with your R&D team and watch what happens."

Today's products don't necessarily *sell themselves*. (If you have one that does, then you've hit a homerun.) Today's successful products are *embedded with a story* that speaks to a niche audience. It was during this era that Nike told the world to "Just Do It" (1988). Apple asked us to "Think different" (1997). These brands created an identity that consumers *wanted* to be associated with. They didn't tell us to join them. Rather, they showed us a better way of being ourselves. To meet our potential, all we had to do was buy a pair of Nike running shoes or an Apple computer.

The *story* that Nike embedded into its advertisements – through words, photos, video, and sponsorships – was one worth grabbing onto. Nike told us to work hard, to have dreams and goals, to push ourselves on to greater heights – even when no one else around us was willing to join. Nike told us that we *mattered* and that we could become anything we wanted to be. All we had to was get out there and train. Run *faster*. Jump *higher*. Be the best. Anyone can do it; it just takes work – work that most people aren't willing to put in. But you? *You're different*, said Nike. *Just do it.*

A story like Nike's holds incredible persuasive power. You only have to see one good Nike commercial or magazine ad to understand their story. They don't have to tell you to buy their product, because you've already imagined yourself into the commercial. Take, for example, Nike's 2012 'Greatness' TV spot[36], featuring a single long take of an overweight teenager running on a rural road:

"Greatness," says the voiceover. "It's just something we made up. Somehow we've come to believe that greatness is a gift reserved for a chosen few. For prodigies. For superstars. And the rest of us can only stand by watching. You can forget that. Greatness is not some rare DNA strand. It's not some precious thing. Greatness is no more unique to us than breathing. We're all capable of it. All of us."

Now *that's* a powerful story.

It was during the 1980s-2000s era that targeted messaging (also: "permission marketing" and – similar – "content marketing") began its rise to prominence. Mass messages for mass audiences began to fail. (Even Nike, after all, isn't speaking to *everybody*.) To quote Seth Godin again, "Permission marketing is the privilege (not the right) of delivering anticipated, personal and relevant messages to people who actually want to get them."[37]

Slowly but surely, the idea of tailoring very specific messages for very specific audiences – audiences who *want* to hear what you have to say – began to gain traction. The internet cracked open a world of small tribes and niche markets, who could now connect with one another outside of time and space constraints.

Advertisers had a host of new data capabilities and tools to reach these niche markets. But some of the most impressive feats in brand communications were still to come. The stagnant brand-to-consumer flow of conversation was soon to be upended and *extended*, consumer-to-consumer. Brands would no longer be the sole gatekeepers of information; nor would they be the only salespeople for their product. The consumer's power was about to be made manifest in the Age of Influence.

2000S-PRESENT: THE AGE OF INFLUENCE

Prior to the internet, consumers were fairly limited in their options for evaluating a product or company. You could call up your local Better Business Bureau, pick up a copy of *Consumer Reports*, or phone a friend. Otherwise, product/service information came your way via the salesperson.

The internet changed all of that. Brand communications were no longer top-down. With the web, the exchange of information became a peer-to-peer process (to employ a Dot-com Bubble-era term). Consumer-oriented websites, forums, review aggregators, bloggers, and online product demos developed across all industries. If you wanted to *really know* how good a product was... all you had to do was ask. Chances are, someone had already tried it, and shared their experience.

In 2004, Yelp (the now-famous online review platform) launched with $1 million in the bank. Ten years later, the site is valued at $5 billion and receives 130 million unique visitors per month.[38] Likewise, new products have lived and died at the hands of Amazon customers, whose reviews hold far more influence than any product description the manufacturer could hope to write.

In the Age of Influence, it's the *customer's voice* – not the *brand's* – that carries the most weight.

But the *real* power of the consumer came with the rise of social media. There's no better product endorsement than a friend or family member's social media post. According to a survey[39] that included 24,000 social media-connected consumers...

> • 88 percent of respondents said that they would trust a friend or family member who received a free product in exchange for a review.

THE **SMART** BRANDS

know they don't hold
yesterday's power.

———

THE **SMARTER** BRANDS

extract the power of
user-generated content.

———

THE **SMARTEST** BRANDS

equip users with tools
for creating content.

• 78 percent would trust a blogger who received a free product for a review.

• "Trust" in product recommendations has increased year-to-year on Facebook, Pinterest, and YouTube.

• In 2014, more consumers used Facebook, blogs, Pinterest, and Instagram to discover new brands and services than they did a "brand-owned community" (i.e. that brand's social account).

I call our current era of brand communications "The Age of Influence." Brands no longer hold the same authority that they did in the Mass Broadcasting/*Mad Men* era. Today, the power is totally in the consumer's hands. This is why so many brands invest in user-generated content, influencer marketing, and hashtag-fueled campaigns that only work when passionate fans are engaged in the conversation.

Without the fans, the campaigns flop. And without *authenticity*, there are no fans.

The **smart** brands know they don't hold yesterday's power.

The **smarter** brands extract the power of user-generated content.

The **smartest** brands equip users with tools for creating content.

In the Age of Influence, brands no longer control what is said about them or how they are perceived. No amount of budget or creativity can cover up the truth.

In the Age of Influence, **story** is everything. Sure, "storytelling" is a buzzword in today's marketing culture, but it's a buzzword for a reason: *it works.* Today's great brands are great storytellers. They know how to weave a narrative that's true and authentic to whom they are. Their narrative is a part of everything that they do. We'll talk more about being genuine and using storytelling as a technique in chapter five.

Arguably one of the most authentic means of storytelling in The Age of Influence is "influencer marketing." *Forbes* contributor Kyle Wong defines influence marketing as, "a form of marketing that identifies and targets individuals with influence over potential buyers."[40]

In essence, influencer marketing is sort of like the old-fashioned "celebrity endorsement." It's no new concept – not by any means – but it does push the envelope a little further. David Ogilvy, one of the *Mad Men*-era advertising greats, once wrote, "[Testimonials by celebrities] are below average in their ability to change brand preference. Viewers guess the celebrity has been bought, and they are right. Viewers have a way of remembering the celebrity while forgetting the product." [41]

As our culture has only been increasingly bombarded by advertisements, I would argue that disinterest in celebrity testimonials is even greater than it was in Ogilvy's day...

...which is where influencer marketing comes in. "Influencers," in this sense, may or may not be celebrities. More often than not, they are people who hold significant sway with a small group of people: teenaged YouTube heartthrobs, mommy bloggers, tech journalists, and indie filmmakers. They're "mini-celebrities" in their own right, which – in the ad business – offers a lot more ROI than a LeBron James or Leonardo DiCaprio.

Influencers offer immense value because they already have the audience. Typically, their audience has been built through an authentic portrayal of themselves, a strong cause/message, and a keen understanding of their audience's heart. When an influencer "markets" a product (which may be as casual as posting a photo of them using the product), audiences respond much more favorably than they would to a plainly obvious "celebrity endorsement."

According to a 2015 study of influence marketing[42], **92 percent** of consumers trust recommendations from other people (even someone they don't know) over branded content.

In another study[43] (referenced earlier), researchers found that **83 percent** of respondents said that personal stories made a review or recommendation influential. The "number of reviews" and "number of comments on the post" mattered relatively little by comparison.

My point is not that you should have everyone else do your marketing *for you*. Rather, I want you to see the shift in thinking that's occurred over the last 100 years, and know...

WE HAVE A REASON TO CELEBRATE.

Gradually, we have seen brand communications transition from an industry that blanketed a mass audience with guilt and fear *(coercing the sale)* to an industry that's focused on enriching the lives of very specific people through beautiful stories and engaging ideas.

That's something to celebrate.

We have more tools at our disposal for **telling stories** and **enriching people** now than ever before. How do we bend ourselves to this perspective? How do we do it effectively? And why? We'll explore all of these questions in the next few pages...

RESTORING

OUR DIGITAL

ENVIRONMENT

"A pile of rocks ceases to be a rock pile when somebody contemplates it with the idea of a cathedral in mind."
— Antoine de Saint-Exupéry

Purpose is a remarkable thing. It's the fuel behind creativity's fire. It's the cool drink of water that replenishes the entrepreneur when he thinks about closing up shop and working for someone else. Purpose is what grounds us and gives us energy to keep doing the work set out before us.

It doesn't matter how inspired, industrious, or intelligent a person is... if they lack purpose in their work, then their capacity for success will have a low ceiling. Purpose is the secret ingredient.

We live in a fascinating time where everyone with an internet connection and a computer has – more or less – "resource equality." Today's digital culture levels the playing field by offering high-powered tools to both the Fortune 500 company and the garage startup. Open-source software, social media networks, affordable creative platforms, and robust analytic/tracking tools allow everyone equal access. If you have a problem, there's a good chance someone has built the solution, and it's either free or affordable.

But *purpose* is the one thing that can't be bought, given, or learned. You've either found it or you haven't.

The individual with purpose approaches these tools – or de Saint-Exupéry's "pile of rocks" – and desires to create something new and wonderful with them. There's a deep power in these tools when they're perceived as more than just time-savers and revenue-generators, but viewed as apps and programs for achieving that ultimate piece of the puzzle... *purpose*.

OUR PURPOSE IS RESTORATION.

As I've said before, I consider **restoration** to be one of my primary purposes as a professional. I like the Antoine de Saint-Exupéry quote above for how it marries *purpose* and *restoration*. A driven individual is able to cut through the noise, identify the necessary tools, and layer them so as to achieve a clear purpose: building a beautiful cathedral.

His metaphor moves in two directions. On the one hand, his imagined observer is able to view the rock pile as a cathedral. On the other hand, though, the very act of *imagining* a cathedral transforms the pile of rocks themselves. Note his language: "...*ceases* to be a rock pile..."

By simply *considering* the building blocks in a different way, we ascribe value to them. The blocks are imbued with purpose – no longer a pile of rubble. What aspect of your own career or business would change if you began viewing it as *purposeful* as opposed to "rubble?" How would a *restorative* outlook affect the way you see your purpose on the macro-level (i.e. your career path) and on the micro-level (i.e. Monday morning staff meetings)?

WHY RESTORATION? WHY NOW?

Why am I so interested in restoration? As I see it, we restore because we believe in the **value of people** and because **we have the ability** to make them *feel* that value. Restoration is a method of validation, a way of making someone *feel* his or her true worth.

In his *Harvard Business Review* essay, "The Only Thing that Really Matters,"[44] Tony Schwartz writes, "To feel valued (and valuable) is almost as compelling a need as food. The more our value feels at risk, the more preoccupied we become with defending and restoring it, and the less value we're capable of creating in the world." Validation isn't just a "nice thing" to give someone. It's not something we do to make others feel better or boost our own egos. It's a real need that we all feel deep down within ourselves.

Schwartz cites several studies and anecdotes related to our deep inner-desire – "our core emotional need" – to feel valued. But perhaps one of the most compelling examples in his essay comes from Doug Conant, former CEO of Campbell Soup:

> Over the past decade, Conant has spent at least an hour a day writing between 10 and 20 handwritten notes to people in his company — welcoming new hires, thanking employees for their contributions, and congratulating leaders for specific accomplishments.

> "Toughness on issues, tenderness with people," is Conant's mantra.

If a bottom-line-driven businessman with dozens of other more pressing issues on his desk takes an hour a day *just to make his employees feel valued,* then shouldn't that inform our perspectives on value and validation? Most of us aren't playing with Fortune 500 chips like Conant, and yet we

IT DOESN'T MATTER HOW
INSPIRED, INDUSTRIOUS, OR
INTELLIGENT A PERSON IS...

IF THEY LACK PURPOSE IN
THEIR WORK, THEN THEIR
CAPACITY FOR SUCCESS WILL
HAVE A LOW CEILING.

PURPOSE IS THE SECRET
INGREDIENT.

still consider ourselves too busy to prioritize the feelings of our employees, customers, and audience.

Validation is one of the most effective things we can do for our audience. While "feeling valued" has been revealed in multiple studies to be linked with well-being and performance[45], there's also something undeniably good, noble, and desirable in making another person feel valid and valued. So, how do you start?

We start by restoring. And we start now. We begin out of an assumption that people aren't accustomed to feeling like they're cared for. While we've all become used to great customer service and perks like "Free Shipping & Returns" in certain sectors, we definitely don't *expect* these things from every business. It took brands like Zappos, Amazon, and REI a long time to develop their customer service policies before they earned the trust of millions of customers.

Many companies are still stuck in a way of thinking that predates those examples. If you look back on the last 100 years of brand communications, you can clearly trace out a pattern that, by and large, says, "We don't care about you." From false ideals in advertising to mass broadcasting's loud mouth, brands don't have the strongest track record with ascribing *value* to actual individual human beings.

This is why I believe that the time for restoration is *now*. The tides are turning. Many brands have already started the long process of validating their employees, customers, and audience. It's time for everyone else to follow suit... or, better yet, **lead**. As I noted earlier in this chapter, the tools of restoration are cheap – if not *free* – and available to everyone. If you have a computer and an internet connection, you can start now.

While I greatly admire Doug Conant's very specific and very tangible method of validating his employees, I'd like to cast an even wider net in this book. Let's look at how brands can use digital means to restore entire audiences in the thousands or even *millions*.

RESTORATION MADE POSSIBLE

Not Impossible Labs

Mick Ebeling is a man who can look at a pile of rocks and see a cathedral. In 2010, he built the Eyewriter, a pair of eye-tracking glasses that allowed a paralyzed graffiti artist to draw using only his eyes. In 2013, moved by a story of Sudanese refugees, he bought a plane ticket and travelled to Yida in South Sudan, where he used 3D-printing technology to develop prosthetic limbs for those who had lost arms and legs in the conflict.

If the story ended there, it would be an impressive case of charity. But Ebeling went one step further; he gifted the village with the 3D printer and *taught the people* – many of whom had never even used a computer before – how to create their own prosthetics.

"I don't believe that you can fix someone," says Ebeling. "That was never my goal here. [...] You can't put the pieces back together in someone else's life. But maybe if we print them new pieces, they'll start to learn to put them back together themselves."[46]

Ebeling acknowledged the Other's humanity. He didn't enter as a savior; he didn't throw out free prizes. He provided a service that recognized the dignity in other people. He had faith in the intelligence, skill, and capacity of his "audience" when he taught them how to use the 3D printer themselves. In other words, he used technology and today's digital capabilities to *restore* what was broken in these people.

Of course, there's another layer entirely to Ebeling's work. Not Impossible Labs doesn't just affect the refugees on the ground in Sudan. It also affects us. In addition to doing his work in Sudan, Ebeling went the extra mile, partnering with Intel to produce "Project Daniel" web and video content, a book *(Not Impossible: The Art and Joy of Doing What Couldn't Be Done)*, and a blog highlighting the latest innovative products and ideas that are "hacking technology for the sake of humanity" (www.notimpossiblenow.com).

Ebeling teaches us that restoring people and their environments is more than just showing up and fixing a problem; it involves validating them, recognizing their dignity, and empowerment. Restoration is a *purposeful* process through which a community is created and nourished.

Lowe's

Lowe's is one of my favorite examples of a "restorative" brand because it's an unexpected one. Lowe's extends their company slogan, "Never Stop Improving," all the way out to their digital presence. Their digital content is creative and fresh, while their brand is one of the most responsive (and friendly) on social media.

If you look at Lowe's Facebook page[47], you'll witness an excellent example of *two-way conversation*. Lowe's doesn't just broadcast messages; they also don't put out garbage content. The social media team behind the Lowe's Facebook page takes great care to answer each and every Facebook comment that voices an idea or opinion. (No one can expect them to respond to all of the *hundreds* of Facebook comments they get every day.)

Lowe's responses are personal and genuine, always affirming the commenter and giving next-level service. I've observed the following systems Lowe's has in place:

- Issues are often resolved within Facebook Post comment threads.

- If an issue cannot be resolved publicly on Facebook, then the Lowe's team will suggest the user email carefb@lowes.com with a unique case number subject line that will allow the email customer service representative to read through the issue.

- As an alternative, Lowe's directs customers to its Rant or Rave App on Facebook[48], where customers can submit their stories and complaints to appear publicly on the Facebook page app. A quick scan through Rant or Rave will show multiple instances of Lowe's taking prompt action to resolve customer issues. The app also includes many incendiary "raves," some of which no doubt, are grounded in some ugly truth. This is one way Lowe's is able to promote authenticity and genuine communication.

In all of these customer interactions, Lowe's validates customers. Responses begin with phrases like, "We understand how that can be frustrating..." When customers have something to celebrate or an interesting fact to share, the Lowe's social team shows genuine interest and asks follow-up questions. Users are thanked for their ideas and contributions. In short, people are made to feel *valued* when they interact with Lowe's on Facebook.

While Lowe's is great at social response, they do a terrific job with content creation, as well. The home improvement chain was an early adopter of Vine, Twitter's six-second social video network[49]:

Lowe's joined Vine in May 2013, about 4 months after it launched. We believed the growth in short-form mobile video was about to become mainstream and the creative constraints of Vine intrigued us. We liked the idea of needing to tell incredibly concise brand stories in just 6 seconds- it would force us to have a sharp point and get to it quickly.

...and Lowe's Vines[50] are exactly that. Insightful, witty, interesting, and genuinely helpful, the brand always delivers with their video content. Instead of propping up a talking head and letting the camera roll, Lowe's uses fun stop motion techniques to tell their stories. (Behind-the-scenes details are especially impressive.[51]) You won't believe how entertaining gardening tips and home improvement suggestions can be until you watch their work.

So, maybe you're still wondering how a digital presence like Lowe's translates to "restoration?" If I had to boil it down to one concise sentence, it would be this:

Lowe's respects their audience.

Respect is at the heart of validation. Consumers in our society aren't used to being respected by brands as people. "Politeness" may be *expected*. "Good customer service" may be *expected*. But *respect* as a human – even when you aren't a paying customer – is not yet the norm for consumers. We don't assume that a Top 50 company in the United States is actually going to *care* about us or *validate* us – even if we aren't currently shopping there!

Lowe's respects their audience by taking the time to (a) create content worth watching and (b) meaningfully respond to people who engage with their brand. If every brand acted like Lowe's, then this book wouldn't need a chapter on restoring our digital environment.

Passion Passport

Not Impossible Labs shows us what restoration looks like in a very big, life-impacting way. Lowe's shows us what restoration looks like when you're a gigantic corporation that can hire BBDO to partner with you on creative. What does restoration look like for... the rest of us?

Passion Passport is one of my favorite brands that demonstrates "restoration for the rest of us." Aptly named, Passion Passport is a group that

CONSUMERS

---

in our society

aren't used to being

RESPECTED

by **BRANDS**

as **PEOPLE.**

leverages the passion of travel-lovers to share incredible stories that put life back into its users. The company is a content powerhouse, publishing travel photos, videos, and blogs through a number of digital channels, including social media and its own website.[52] (That being said, Instagram is definitely this brand's hub. At the time of writing, their Instagram account has a following 46x the size of their closely matched Facebook and Twitter accounts.)

Since the beginning (Spring 2013), Passion Passport has been a restorative presence in social media. The company publishes a wide range of user-generated content and hosts a number of contests throughout the year – two practices that have been tremendously helpful in jumpstarting a following.

As its following has grown, Passion Passport has gained the leverage to develop partnerships with PayPal, Amtrak, and other large brands. These partnerships have allowed for monetization, further exposure, and – perhaps most importantly for this brand – the ability to gift travelers and photographers with unique experiences and amazing trips.

Passion Passport is *restorative* in that the company puts a priority on *people*. (Its mission, after all, is "to elevate the conversation from talking about **things** to talking about **experiences**.") Perhaps the best example of this people-first focus is the Passport Express, a partnership between Passion Passport and Amtrak that sent 25 Instagram photographers and nine mentors on a cross-country train ride together. The trip presented massive exposure and growth opportunity for both sponsors by maximizing their guests' own social media audiences. And yet... audiences could fully enjoy the Passport Express's photos and stories without feeling as if they were being spoon-fed a sponsored event.

The team at Passion Passport knows how to balance brand messaging with authentic storytelling and a true appreciation of their audience. Passion Passport *respects* their audience; they give; they validate. Perhaps this is one reason why Passion Passport has grown to 540k Instagram followers in less than three years.

WHAT WILL YOU BUILD WITH THE TOOLS YOU HAVE?

The periodic table contains 118 unique elements. These 118 gases, solids, and liquids make up every physical thing in existence. Remarkably, there are collectors who have actually assembled sets of these 118 elements. In a box no bigger than a briefcase you can fit the building blocks of the world. Every natural or artificial item to have ever existed, from fighter jets to ancient stalactites is contained within this little briefcase.

Once again, I'm reminded of Antoine de Saint-Exupéry's quote about the pile of rocks. Once we begin to see the elements with *purpose*, they cease to be a pile of rocks, and are instilled with infinite value.

I imagine that if you ever had the chance to gaze into one of those collector's briefcases, you would feel a sense of wonder, awe, and possibility. Through zillions of unique combinations these elements hold the answers to so many of our problems. The physical elements can be rearranged to solve very *non*-physical problems like loneliness and low self-esteem... poverty... damaged relationships... and much more. Ebeling used them to give someone an arm. Lowe's used them to brighten someone's day. Passion Passport used them to give somebody the trip of a lifetime and inspire millions.

I've called myself a "technology optimist" before, and this has both benefits and drawbacks. But perhaps the strongest 'pro' tick on this viewpoint's pro/con list is that it's a viewpoint driven by hope. In order to be authentically optimistic about today's technology, it's essential to hold fast to hope – to be *driven* by **intent** and **purpose** to restore brokenness in humanity.

Today, all of us have access to the digital version of those 118 elements. The very building blocks of the web – the tools of communication – are in our pockets and on our desks: codes, browsers, hardware, systems... all of the elements for creating *anything* are available to us.

I think I get to experience some version of the sense of awe attached to looking at the 118 elements when I sit down at my own desk. The tools are many; the purposes are few and concise. That's where the magic happens. When we have **purpose** and a heart to restore, that "pile of rocks" can become much, much more than what it shows itself to be at first glance.

THE HUMAN

IMPRINT

How can you make people feel "validated" and "restored" as a brand? ... organization? ...corporation? How are you supposed to sound personal? *Human?* These are tough questions that come up when you propose a totally new way of seeing the relationship between brands and people.

Today, the distinction between "brands" and "people" is fading as an increasing number of brands become so adept at communicating online that – for all intents and purposes – they sound like an actual person you want to be friends with. We are rapidly approaching a tipping point where successful, purposeful, restorative brands *must* communicate with a **distinctly human imprint** in order to make it in today's digital environment. Those who don't cross over to this way of communicating will soon be perceived as abrasive and out-of-touch as a poorly produced car dealer's commercial.

THE FALSE DICHOTOMY: BRAND V. HUMAN

We've been lied to.

We've been told that there should be a difference between who we are as companies, brands, startups, non-profits, and organizations...

...and who we are online.

When we're at work, we are professional, fun, easy-going, or stressed, but when we're posting to social media, we have to be *all-business-all-the-time*. We have to be dead serious. No gray areas. Nothing we say or do should ever run the risk of being misconstrued as offensive.

...so goes one lie.

Here's another:

At work, we are focused. We are professionals. We work with serious clients on serious matters: finance, law, medicine, etc. But on social media, we're expected to cut-up, be goofy, and post content that will make people think we're fun.

Again, it's a lie.

This way of thinking is a classic example of a false dichotomy. We have been told that we must have either personality A or personality B on social media. We must portray ourselves to be a fun and lighthearted brand or we must be strictly professional. There is no in-between or switching back-and-forth. There's none of that gray area that's so core to the human experience. It's an either-or scenario, we're told.

The truth is, this way of thinking is flawed; the world has much more gray area than these stereotypes can accommodate. This way of thinking fails to take into account the complexity of **who we are as people** – to say nothing of the complexities of our *human* audiences. There is a way forward between this binary line of thought. There is a middle ground that doesn't merely compromise, but is actually more authentic and realistic then choosing between A and B.

YOU'RE SO COMPLICATED... AND SO IS YOUR COMPANY.

People are complex. Nobody is ever completely serious or a total goofball. We all straddle a line, wavering between two extremes: polite v. rude, kind v. mean, introverted v. extroverted, happy v. sad. Very few people are 100% one and 0% the other. We all fluctuate depending on our mood, situation, stress levels, social life, etc.

Depending on your own personality, you may feel free to express this fluctuation at work, or you might feel the need to bottle it up and wear your game face to the office everyday, no matter what's going on inside. For most of us, though, our mood affects our work to some noticeable degree.

The collective "mood" of a company is a large part of what makes up that company's *culture*, along with the company's vision, values, and beliefs. "Mood" and "company culture" tend to stabilize. They can fluctuate when business is good or when sales are down or when there's significant leadership turnover. But, for the most part, company culture remains more or less the same. Your organization may be optimistic, innovative, determined, competitive... these are all words that could be used to describe an organization's core mood or *culture*. There are likely outliers within your organizations, as well as small, gradual shifts in direction. But, for the most part, a company's culture should be solid and understood by everyone in it.

Your brand in the digital space should be an expression of this company culture. If we're being honest with ourselves, that company culture proba-bly includes some polar opposites. Take, for example, these phrases that are often thrown around in company culture documents:

- *Work hard, play hard.*

- *Big risk, big reward.*

- *Creative thinking, managed process.*

Work too hard, and you might not have time to play.

Take too much risk, and you might lose it all.

Put too much emphasis on creative thinking, and project management can become a nightmare.

...you get the idea. All company cultures, whether or not they employ these sometimes-paradoxical statements, are a balancing act.

TWO COMMON WAYS FOR A BRAND TO APPEAR DEAD

Okay, we can probably all agree that we're a little complex as human beings. So, back to the original question: why do we believe this lie that our digital and social presence should have *singular* personalities? I would argue that many people buy into this myth because **they perceive a digital presence as being lifeless.** Here's what I mean by that...

Your website, your social media, your email blasts... these forms of communication can all be packed up neatly. They can be produced in advance, automated, and directed at a highly targeted audience with specific objectives in mind. Many people have difficulty seeing their digital presence as anything more than a means to an end. So, in order to achieve their business goals – whether that's more sales, product line expansion, or breaking into a new market, they **stick to "the persona."** They play a conservative game by defining a singular voice that knows *one way of communication.*

And the audience doesn't go for it. It sounds flat. Fake. Inauthentic. Simply... *not human.*

WE ALL STRADDLE A LINE,

WAVERING BETWEEN

TWO EXTREMES:

POLITE V. RUDE

KIND V. MEAN

INTROVERTED V. EXTROVERTED

HAPPY V. SAD

VERY FEW PEOPLE ARE 100%

ONE AND 0% THE OTHER.

Why? Because that's not how people act. Serious people can be funny, upbeat people have a bad day, and so on.

On the other end of the spectrum, you have companies who treat their brand's digital presence as nothing more than a listicle-regurgitator. This oftentimes happens with companies who know just enough to "know they should be on social media," but don't know how to behave or what to share on those social media profiles. A common problem with these brands is that they *think* they don't have any original content to share, whether that's ideas, stories, photos, videos, blogs, etc.

Like the companies who run a tight sales game on social media, these "content regurgitation brands" come off sounding dead and lifeless. Both companies reach the same conclusion by taking opposite routes.

YOUR DIGITAL PRESENCE AS AN EXPRESSION OF YOU

I encourage my clients to see their digital presence as an expression of *themselves*, whether they're solopreneurs or large corporations. Find the pulse in your organization – the "company culture" – and play with it online. Explore all of its corners, how it's expressed in good times and bad, how it relates with peers, customers, and competitors.

Do this, and you'll find that your brand is suddenly much more "human" and *real* online than you thought. The notion that your company's online presence must be all-business or all-personal is a myth. Furthermore, it's a deception that you don't have enough original content to post. Below, we'll take a look at a few brands who have digital personalities that mix and match a variety of different "moods" in order to reflect an authentic company culture. We'll also look at how these brands create their content, dispelling the false belief that you don't have the collateral to put together great content for *your* brand.

BIG CORPORATION: TACO BELL

Taco Bell is one of those big Fortune 500 companies that can be completely off-the-wall, but *perfectly* so. As one of the fastest growing franchises in North America[53], Taco Bell is going full speed-ahead for the Millennial/Gen Z market. (They've always thought young, being the first fast food company to partner with a major movie blockbuster – *Batman* in 1989.[54])

Taco Bell's company voice is fun, witty, lighthearted, and has a tight, symbiotic relationship with its audience that is rarely accomplished by other brands. Their website design (tacobell.com or ta.co) says it all. A big homepage promotes the latest product rollout, while a very small and compact website menu offers just three options: Food, Locations, and The Feed. The first two menu items are obvious; the third offers stories, interviews, and other exclusive content that strengthens brand awareness and engenders brand loyalty.

What does Taco Bell actually sound like?

> • **404 Page**[55]: THE PAGE YOU WERE LOOKING FOR DOES NOT EXIST (Unless you were looking for a page with an animation of a taco tripping and literally spilling the beans. in which case, it definitely exists, and you definitely found it.) *(Page accompanied by such an animation.)*

> • **"Senior Picture Goals"**[56]: A Facebook post about a girl who took her senior pictures at Taco Bell — something that sounds exactly like a promotion Taco Bell would have come up with if they thought of it first.

> • **Customer Poll**[57]: "Serious question: What would you do to bring back the Beefy Crunch Burrito? No promises," says one Facebook post.

Playful, light, and innovative. As Fast Company suggests, "All across adland, marketers talk about embracing the ethos of startups—but Taco Bell has become the unlikely innovator that's actually done it."[58] Taco Bell doesn't just try to *connect with* or *act like* Millennials; their voice *is* the Millennial voice.

I'm in no way suggesting that all corporations should be playful or try to act like Millennials online. However, Taco Bell is a terrific example of how a large corporation can defy stereotypes by genuinely communicating in a surprising and fresh way.

PERSONAL VENTURES: JON ACUFF & GARY VAYNERCHUK

Jon Acuff is a *New York Times* bestselling-author, who has worked with The Home Depot, Bose, Staples, and the Dave Ramsey Team. Today, he's his large social media following, speaking engagements, and writings, which more-or-less focus on helping people learn how to love the work they do.

Gary Vaynerchuk – also known as "Gary Vee" – is a fast-talking, spitballing leader in social media, who began his career with the Wine Library, "the Internet's leading discount wine retailer." Vaynerchuk made his mark in 2006 when he launched WineLibraryTV[59], a YouTube channel that entertained and educated audiences about various aspects of wine and wine tasting.

While these two guys have different messages and communication styles on the surface, they do share one thing in common: they are both *excellent* at conveying their brand's voice in the digital space. Acuff and Vaynerchuk masterfully walk the lines between personal and public, professional and relaxed, and humorous and serious.

Acuff can throw a social media curve ball that dances into all the corners of his voice. Take, for example, a post[60] he shared to Instagram: a screenshot from an article he wrote for *Time*. The accompanying caption is simple:

"Writing for @time has been one of the most enjoyable things I've done this year. I still can't believe they let me share ideas like this one. (Tag the friend who won't let you date idiots.)"

The caption is engaging ("can't believe they let me share ideas like this one"), there's a clear and fun call-to-action that helps amplify his reach ("Tag the friend who won't let you date idiots."), and the little bit of writing in the screenshot is amusing, true, and valuable all at once. The post has absolutely nothing to do with his latest career book, *Do Over,* but the self-improvement content is perfect crossover material for an audience already interested in making their professional lives better. If Acuff's audience can trust him on something they already know and have experience with – dating – then they can probably trust him in another area of life: career.

If Acuff is your goofy, fun big brother... then Vaynerchuk is the crass smart aleck slouching in the back row of the class. (Both are brilliant.) His content covers a wide range of topics, from the New York Jets to wine to social media to startup investment. Vaynerchuk's voice varies widely, making him an excellent example of how a brand can show two sides of a coin while still remaining the *same* coin.

Take, for example, two videos shared within two days of each other. In the first video, Episode 149 of the #AskGaryVee Show[61], we see the fast-

MANY PEOPLE HAVE

DIFFICULTY SEEING THEIR DIGITAL

PRESENCE AS ANYTHING MORE THAN A

MEANS TO AN END.

talking, straight-to-the-point, jugular-throbbing Vaynerchuk standing outside in a square in London. This Vaynerchuk variation is the one that most of his fans would recognize. His energy level is high. In the second untitled video[62], Vaynerchuk sits calmly at a board table and lays out some of the key directions he sees consumer trends moving in the future. The videos are equally engaging and have the same personality, but are distinctly different in their mood and pace. Vaynerchuk is a master in this you haven't seen his content before, I encourage you to go check him out to get a feel for the variations yourself.

The bottom line: brands can and should be creative in displaying different versions of their brand. The very best brands don't stick to *single expressions* of their voice. The best brands are able to act like human beings, expressing their ideas and messages in different ways that are appropriate to the audience.

COMMUNICATING IN A CONTENT-SATURATED WORLD

If you've felt discouraged about the challenges of portraying your company culture, I hope these examples have offered at least a glimmer of hope. It *can* be done, and practice and experience certainly help. In the following chapters we'll look at very tangible, hands-on ways to execute these concepts. But there's still one big question that remains:

Who cares?

You learn how to share your brand online. You discover the voice. You figure out how to create your own original content... but who cares? Why is anyone going to listen or be excited about what you have to say?

Seth Godin refers to our era as an "Attention Economy."[63] Today's companies traffic in attention. Amazon wants to get and keep our attention, so that when you need to buy something, you're already thinking of them first. Netflix wants to attract your attention, so that when you finish one TV series, you naturally start looking around on Netflix for your *next* show.

These brands know that we are all totally saturated with content. There are more products, services, writers, producers, musicians, apps, electronics, and opportunities than ever before! We are being pulled in a million directions at once. Attention is a scarce and precious commodity. If a brand can get it, then they've won most of the battle.

But – and this is a big "but" – "Every interaction comes with a cost," Godin reminds us. Waste a person's attention "with spam, with a worthless offer, with a lack of preparation, and yes, with nervous dissembling, then you are unlikely to get another chance."

People don't give freely of their attention. We can only allocate so much of it to each thing that interests us. For me, one Amazon promotional email a week is okay, but one every two weeks is more in-line with the level of attention I'm willing to give. An Amazon email every day? I'm going to unsubscribe in a hurry.

One of the challenges of communicating in a content-saturated world is that brands have to be able to determine (a) whose attention is worth getting, and (b) how much they are willing to spend to *get* that attention. As Godin writes, "Attention is a bit like real estate, in that they're not making any more of it. Unlike real estate, though, it keeps going up in value."[64] In other words, an increasing number of products, services, and creators will be clamoring for our attention in the future; at the same time, people find what they like and develop their loyalties. Attention becomes increasingly scarce.

The cost of obtaining consumer attention becomes higher as more brands learn how to create engaging content. For example, ten years ago, a person who had a firm understanding of their company voice and what makes for "good content" would have a pretty good shot at owning the #1 Facebook page for their lawn care business. Today there are possibly hundreds of lawn care businesses in your city with Facebook pages. It takes a lot more effort to be excellent because of content saturation. Attention has become scarcer.

Of course, lawn care is only one of *hundreds* of services clamoring for consumer attention. What does it take to break through the noise today? Here's how to answer that tough, "Who cares?" question...

1) Is my brand's online voice a genuine expression of our company culture?

2) Am I creating content that's valuable/useful/helpful/interesting to my audience?

3) Am I being restorative?

"yes" to those three questions, you will get people's

 ʝre. At least, the *right* people will care. Very, very few brands
 of those marks. Many brands have figured out the first two, but
ʝ⌐   ̩earned how to restore and validate their audience *as people*. Do
these ⌐ ̩ee things, and your message will resonate.

If you're struggling with the idea of "restoration," here are some benchmarks to consider:

• Is my content leaving my audience better than I found them?

• Does my content improve my audience's perception of the platform I used to communicate the message?

• Has my content encouraged/uplifted/inspired/helped my audience?

• Is my content connecting people who need to know each other?

• Is my content giving more than it's taking (in time, money, or mood)?

HOW TO THRIVE IN THE ATTENTION ECONOMY

The Attention Economy is a tough place to make it as a brand. I believe there are **four core areas** brands have to focus on in order to communicate well and effectively restore what traditional advertising and marketing has stripped of us... our humanity. In the next four chapters, we will take a closer look at these behaviors:

• Be genuine.

• Lay your cards down: transparency.

• Respond frequently and thoroughly.

• Embrace the ratings/reviews environment.

In closing, remember these things: The idea that there must be a differen͜ between how brands and humans communicate in the digital space is simply not true. Brands can be genuinely human in the way they express their voice and through the type of content they publish. Not only does behavior resonate with audiences in the Attention Economy, it can actually go as far as to *restore* the traditional broken relationship that's built up between brands and consumers over the last 100 years. In order to get your audience's attention, you'll need to perfect the above four behaviors, which we will discuss in the next chapters.

BE GENUINE:
KEEP DOIN' YOU

Being genuine isn't the most natural thing to do at work. If we're... well, genuine... we may admit that fear is one of the top motivating factors behind our behavior. We fear shame. We fear failure. We fear that we'll be seen as a fraud. We fear losing our job. We bear a *host of fears* on our back. Some are rational... others less so.

Being *genuine* before our co-workers, customers, and broader audience might expose all of those things that our trusty, reliable "sense of fear" covers up! In some instances, "being genuine" is the scariest behavior of all. So, instead, we find it's much easier to let fear climb into the driver's seat. We can trust that healthy fear of exposure to keep us moving forward. And if a little bit of our authentic self gets buried along the way, well, that's just the cost of doing business, right?

Wrong. Obviously, being controlled by fear is an unhealthy way to live. Fear keeps us from growth; it keeps us from connecting with others. **Ultimately, fear keeps us from following our purpose: restoration.** Fear doesn't just affect your brand and purpose. It is also guaranteed to affect how people perceive your company. Silence and boring conservatism on social media – neither of which are blatant "bad behaviors" – are indicators of fear. These practices, whether we realize it or not, reveal that we are afraid to show a genuine self. We fear putting aside the mask that keeps us safe from potential criticism.

It's time to put that fear away and share our genuine selves. **Vulnerability is currency in the Attention Economy.** Entrepreneur and filmmaker Casey Neistat is among those who has **realized** and **acted** on this core truth.

In the summer of 2015, Neistat ambitiously launched Beme, a live video-streaming social network that upends the way we think about social media. In the product introduction video, Neistat lays out the fundamental problem with social media as he sees it: "Social media is supposed to be a digital version of who we are as people. Instead, it's this highly sculpted, calculated, calibrated version of who we are told through filters that make our eyes bluer."[65]

Many people use social media to project how they want to be seen by the world... instead of how *they* see the world. Filters allow us to enhance our world. Retakes let us show our lives in the very best light. For Neistat and many others, this is an issue. Social media is a construct that blocks us from fully experiencing the moment, he would probably say. It creates false ideals and encourages us to be dishonest about our own lives.

With Beme, users simply hold their phone up to their chest, which automatically starts recording video. That video is then published live – without review or editing by the user – to the Beme network. Other users can video their own responses in real time and reply. Whether or not Beme will change the face of social media remains to be seen. In all honesty, it probably won't. But it's an important idea at an important moment in time.

Beme's significance lies in the fact that it's actively challenging the way we think about connecting with others in the digital space. The app strips away production value and paid promotion, leaving us with nothing but our own real selves. Some journalists have been quick to point out that's boring.[66] But regardless of whether or not the specs of Beme excite you, you have to admit that the shift towards vulnerability in the social space *means something...*

VULNERABILITY: THE TOP COMMODITY IN THE ATTENTION ECONOMY

It's difficult to commit to being *genuine* and to say, "no," to fear. It's a vulnerable way to live. However, this vulnerability that accompanies *genuine* behavior is – and will continue to be – essential for brands in the Attention Economy.

If you are going to ask for something from your audience (i.e. their attention, in whatever form that may be), then you should expect to give something. In the Attention Economy, not all transactions are financial; in fact, *many* are not. The best brands know how to exchange their own vulnerability for their audience's attention.

Being genuine is one of the key behaviors brands must adopt for this age. As we've already discussed, there has been a major shift in the relationship between brands and audiences. Let's do a brief recap of the methods and psychology that dominated the previous 100 years of marketing – and how these methods differ from the way restorative brands communicate today

THE LAST 100 YEARS

The last one hundred years have been primarily concerned with marketers managing what consumers *believe* about a product or service. Even advertising stills like billboards and magazine ads were designed to impress one's imagination more than inform. The public has wised up and assumes that what a brand knows about their products is filtered for advertising. This is less negative than it sounds because everyone accepts the norm of *showing one's better side* and *putting one's best foot forward,* etc. Consumers know and accept that hype is part of the game. This arrangement worked pretty well for brands and marketers in the past because they controlled most of the information to which consumers had access. Service and product sellers had the ability to present their best side and gift wrap their public exposure with slick commercials.

Consumers have been wearied by over a hundred years of information control marketing and almost two generations of mass marketing. To a large extent, marketers have earned the distrust that underscores public cynicism about big business. According to consumer opinion research in 2014, 44% of Americans think advertisements are dishonest.[67]

However, perspectives seem to be changing. – a potential result of more businesses adapting to the realities of the Attention Economy. In 2013, Nielsen released a report comparing consumer trust levels in various forms of advertising. The poll asked for opinions on 19 different types of advertisements, comparing the 2013 data to responses to the same questions asked in 2007. Trust **increased in 12 of the 13 categories** that were represented in both 2007 and 2013. (Newspaper ads were the only form of advertising that saw a dip in trust.) The increase in consumer trust is significant in many categories:

- Text ads on mobile phones: +19% (37% in 2013; 18% in 2007)

- Ads before movies: +18% (56% in 2013; 38% in 2007)

- Online banner ads: +16% (42% in 2013; 26% in 2007)

While consumer trust in brands is on the rise, the same Nielsen poll reminds us that the **most trusted form of advertising** is "recommendations from people I know." Eighty-four percent of consumers put their trust in this form of advertising (up 6% from 78% in 2007).

Marketing technologist Scott Brinker points to graphic data in a similar Nielsen report showing that "50% of consumers neither trust nor distrust advertising regardless of the media/vehicle." For these consumers, Brinker says, the point of advertising is introduction of products and it is the ex

THE MOST TRUSTED

FORM OF ADVERTISING

IS RECOMMENDATIONS

FROM PEOPLE I KNOW.

perience following that builds or damages trust.[69] Brinker's view may be encouraging for brands intent on building trust through experiences with customers. However, it leaves us with the remaining 50% of people, which the Nielsen report suggests is split between those that generally trust advertising and those that don't.

Most advertisers don't outright lie in order to sell a quality product. But let's face it, branding has mostly been about creating an image—how a company wanted to be perceived whether or not the image completely and accurately represented the product. Consumers today are more sophisticated than a generation ago... and they have more tools for ousting a dishonest company. When a false image is uncovered and toppled by consumers, it reinforces a growing resentment toward an all-too-common approach to marketing, the harsh but fair word for which is: *manipulation*. That is the emotion charged perception of mass marketing and sales as a whole. It doesn't matter how different from that perception a particular company may be. One solid principle of human psychology is: whatever is perceived as real *is* real in its consequences.

The only way a brand can now distance itself from the reputation of mass marketing is to abandon it in favor of **genuine behavior and vulnerability.** Image management can no longer be the driving policy of brand promotion. Jamie Monberg of Hornall Anderson makes it clear this way: "If a brand says 'we want to be seen as X,' the correct response from a marketer is 'Are you actually X?' or 'Then go be X,' because no amount of positioning can swing the needle if you aren't actually delivering the experience."[70]

BUYER'S REMORSE AND BLAME SHIFTING

There is another consumer experience that can fan the flames of a dissatisfied consumer's animosity. It has to do with how consumers feel about their purchases. There is a certain amount of personal identity and even guilt playing roles in consumer psychology. Everyone makes emotional decisions about purchases that impact our self-image, which includes most things but especially major purchases like new automobiles. For example, when the first Oldsmobile Cutlasses were delivered to dealers in the early sixties the initial reception was not bad but mostly ho-hum. As American cars went in those days the Cutlass was a well-built car. But it wasn't until GM made a few style changes and through advertising established in the public mind "who" a driver was behind the wheel of the sporty new mid-sized Cutlass that sales exploded and it became for many years a top GM profit maker. The Cutlass was sporty but practical and owners understood how it made them look and feel. And for the most part the car had satisfied owners for decades.

Consumers will forgive themselves for being emotional about certain purchases but they never forget being taken for a ride. The anger they feel after a bad purchase is as much directed at themselves as it is the producer or seller. And it is this aspect of consumer psychology that makes negligence and especially outright deception by a brand all the more self-endangering in our current environment. Consumers want to trust their own judgment. They want to know they can trust what they've been lead to believe about a service or product and that a company will come through for them when they have a problem. How satisfied they eventually are in this regard can be an indicator of a company's ability to be genuine.

It's hard to part with money even for something badly wanted. *Buyer's remorse* is usually about all the other needful things a purchaser is thinking he probably should have spent money on instead of the thing purchased. That's the first experience of guilt. Brands need to be sure they aren't the reason for the second and worse feelings of guilt consumers feel when they decide they've been duped. The stronger the emotions behind a purchase decision, the greater the potential for gain or loss for a company's brand identity. Unhappy and self-accusing consumers have a handy social valve where they can displace their guilt and release their anger. A company that proves deceptive or careless to consumers is going to pay for making them hate themselves by having all the blame shifted their way. But a brand that invests itself to reward their customers' trust by delivering experiences beyond those promised will earn customer loyalty and social media brand advocates.

Quoting Rohit Bhargava, author of *Personality Not Included,* "Every company that consumers are passionate about already understands that sharing an authentic identity inspires loyalty and belief."[71] Brands no longer have time to heal over the impact of negative information with slick ad campaigns and promotions. Now they have to come face to face in conversation with consumers on their turf and have a human face that goes deeper than a smiley mask. They must be *genuine.* They must convincingly say to consumers, "This is who we are and what we are striving to achieve. If we screw up you'll see us bend over backwards to make it right." The only way this can be said convincingly to the current market of jaded and suspicious consumers is to mean it and do it consistently.

The *STRONGER* the

EMOTIONS *behind a*

PURCHASE DECISION,

the GREATER *the*

POTENTIAL *for* GAIN

or LOSS *for a*

company's BRAND

IDENTITY.

Flowing in the main stream of our digital environment has to be raw and unrefined. By definition social media is reality media. Interactions are unrehearsed, unguarded, and real. It's the perfect place to show all factual sides as long as they are the authentic, unpolished, and the strait skinny. Consistent credibility is key for a company's reception and membership in good standing in the social media club. Any veneer, spin, back-peddling, or covering the assets sets a company up for being ignored and distrusted. Off the cuff and face to face, it's very difficult to stage a show. People tend to know in that setting when they're being snowed. So there's no point in a brand coming to the unrehearsed setting of social media until it is comfortable presenting itself as what it really is without makeup or high fashion.

As I wrote at the beginning of this chapter, fear is the natural driving factor behind many behaviors, and the decision to behave genuinely and fearlessly can be... *terrifying*. It feels like a tremendous risk. It's especially difficult to do if you don't feel surrounded by others who are making the same decision. However, the decision to resist the temptation to cover up our true selves and act genuinely instead is absolutely essential for communicating today. More brands will be moving in this direction in the coming years, as social media and multi-touch-point campaigns become even more ingrained into global business practices. Start now, and be a leader. Here are a few tips to get you going...

GUIDELINES FOR BEING
GENUINE & EMBRACING VULNERABILITY

First and foremost, think long-term. Grow your market's recognition of your authenticity the way you expect your kid to earn your trust. It generally takes time but there will be valuable opportunities to leap ahead. Set a policy and only change it to more accurately present your company's authentic identity. Remember our conversation about creating a genuine, human voice from the last chapter.

Don't project a false image. Don't imply your company has a capability that doesn't square with the truth as it is right now. Make sure consumers know who you are, not just who you hope someday to be, and especially not who you merely want consumers to think you are. That may sound like your mother talking, but the forced honesty in social media marketing shows how entrenched deceptive habits have become. Brands are now facing the reality that the unvarnished truth comes out very quickly. So, a vacation spot that advertises an onsite health club better have a lot more than an exercise class in the parking lot if it wants to be competitive for long.

Don't stonewall, sugar coat, or moderate answers to consumer questions and complaints. A moderate tone and manicured reply to something negative doesn't soften the blow for you or your customer. It's just more manipulation and only ticks people off. Or shall I say, it could be perceived, though unintended, as evasive and concealing leading to an unprofitable environment of resistance and discontentment. See the difference? Just keep it real.

Show your fun side not your good side. When we try to show our good side we're thinking about our bad side and anxious to cover it up. Think of it this way: Social media isn't a conference of perfect, beautiful people. In social media we get together with new friends and old to help each other and have fun. When you're genuinely having fun it's hard to be false. Go into it expecting to have a good time with people even when you have to deal with problems. Follow along or even participate in the social media streams of other companies like Southwest Airlines and Coca-Cola to get in the groove of how they make it enjoyable.

Fess up to screw-ups. Do it fast before social media drags it out of you. Nothing will be worse for your authentic brand identity than being outed for covering something up. Bad news doesn't get better with age, so use your social channels to admit what everyone already knows—companies are human institutions and none of them are perfect. Company officers and employees make mistakes and sometimes act foolishly. Even if a screw-up is really bad, if you deal with it quickly, authentically, and with an intent for customer advantage you'll gain from it in the long run. To their credit Microsoft didn't blame shift or downplay the ill-advised tweet about Amy Winehouse. They accepted the guilt, apologized, and in a few weeks the negative buzz died out with minimal lasting impact. In December of 2011, Federal Express had to deal with the very unpleasant impact of a well-circulated video showing a package, containing a video monitor, being tossed over a customer's fence. FedEx wisely responded with emphatic public apologies to the customer and made restitution. Their expression of intolerance for such package handling probably means the deliveryman was immediately looking for another job. Fortunately for FedEx, a long-standing reputation for good service would have limited the lingering impact of the incident. But answering to it quickly and without excuses made it a non-issue and likely resulted in a net gain to consumer confidence.

Every company makes mistakes. If you're lucky, a competitor may even try to kick you when you're down, making you look like the noble underdog. Here's how you respond to that in social media: "It kind of hurt to hear them say that because they're good competitors and we've always admired how they relate to other companies in our industry." Well, maybe that's fudging a little if you don't really admire them, but you get the idea. In communications, it's almost always a good idea to play nice!

LAY YOUR CARDS DOWN: PRACTICING TRANSPARENCY

Transparency is a near relative of genuine and vulnerable behavior in that all of these concepts are measures of honesty. It could be said that *being genuine* has to do with *how* you communicate who you are as a company (i.e. attitude and attention). If that's the case, then *transparency* has more to do with *what* specifically is communicated and to what depth of detail. This is a little trickier because at times determining where the transparency sweet spot is can be situational. If we take the word literally, we are being completely transparent when we hold nothing back. We make public disclosure of everything we have the ability to make known. If that thought makes you sweat, it doesn't necessarily mean something's wrong with you. Transparency at that level can definitely be a scary thing, and is rarely the appropriate choice for any brand. While transparency can be tricky for any company situation, it's especially difficult in the realm of customer service and marketing.

I mentioned before that part of the appeal to social media users is the opportunity it provides for open and personal connection with a larger community without sacrificing independence or control of access. The current development of social media platforms provides gatekeeping tools that allow user-control over how broadly an audience has access to profile information and posts. A Facebook user, for instance, may limit access to friends only or include friends of friends, and even block certain users. That is one technical level of protection from unwanted interaction during personal use of social media.

TRANSPARENCY, TRANSLUCENCY & OPACITY

In social media marketing and customer service, limiting access would be counterproductive. (There are some exceptions when you may want to use Facebook to *only* show certain messages to certain customers.) Therefore, the line has to be drawn somewhere in the string of information. A few rules would help brands decide what policy is honest and appropriate transparency. Marketing veteran and educator Beth Harte suggests understanding *degree of transparency* according to the simple gradients of light transmission we learned in school.

- Letting all the light through unfiltered is being *transparent*.

- Any filtering or diffusing of light is being *translucent*.

- And blocking off transmission of light is being *opaque*.

A company with an *opaque* policy of disclosure or personal engagement will strictly limit interaction with customers to problem solving and scripted replies. A *transparent* customer service policy may perhaps enact call management training to maximize productivity or limit mishaps but won't script or restrict interactions with customers to problem relevance only. It will leave to the service rep's discretion any opportunity he sees to engage personally with the customer and project the company's good will toward the customer's life. A *translucent* policy of interaction with customers will fall somewhere between the two extremes but install limits or filters as the company sees appropriate for its goals and the nature of its business. The assumption here, of course, is that the primary goal of the translucent policy is to enhance customer support and trust and not to conceal information to which a customer would normally feel entitled.[72]

It would be great if success with social media commerce were always just a matter of formulas and patterns like these suggested by Beth Harte. Her categories are useful in a general way for characterizing and communicating a policy. But there will always be situations that challenge the rules and require a bit of wisdom when being transparent, especially with strangers. That's why transparency is as much art as it is science. Transparency goes more deeply to the core of what is human about social media and why people use it. And, of course, this is also why transparency can be tricky.

I like the eloquent way Brian Solis at Altimeter Group describes the delicate balancing act required for meaningful but relevant interaction in social media. He uses the now poplar term "avatar" to mean the personhood we disclose to our online community.

Social media tests the filter that divides inner monologue from disclosure. As our thoughts become words online, they color our avatars and profiles with a glimpse of our personality—who we are online and in the real world. Over time, it is how we put our words into action that establishes our character. And, it is our character, through the marriage of our words and actions, which paves the way for relationships and opportunities.[73]

TRANSPARENCY GOES
MORE DEEPLY TO THE CORE
OF WHAT IS HUMAN ABOUT SOCIAL
MEDIA AND WHY PEOPLE USE IT.

Solis sets a baseline for all of us with this wisdom. The more transparent we are the more color we add to our online personality. But it's only after a time of proven consistency between *what we say and what we do* (how genuine we are) that *who we truly are* emerges to be known and appreciated by the public (character). People, be they friends or customers, are more confident and relaxed with a known quantity.

So let's begin to appreciate the nuances of transparency, at least on principle, by looking at how it can be applied in a few personal and commercial situations. I'll start with a situation described in a Social Media Today article by Beth Harte. Beth was pulled away from her daily online routine for over a week by a death in her family. Many who followed her on Twitter or her popular blog knew of her father-in-law's severe illness but many others began contacting Beth because her absence was so unusual. When she returned online she merely commented that the absence was due to a family situation and left it at that. She comments in the article that the common irrational fear of seeming unprofessional played a part in her reserved choice of words. But, she says, it's a personal decision to choose a level of transparency that is best for each situation. "Not all of us are on the same page for how much transparency is always appropriate."[74] But she also mentions that her father-in-law's obituary was already very public and many people had posted on her blog and tweeted their condolences during the week she was absent. Perhaps instead of evading she could have simply thanked everyone in her return post for the kind condolences about her father-in-law's death and was glad to be back with everyone. That would have been a warm way to connect personally and transparently with her network without diving too deeply into self-indulgent details.

Another social media wiz, Carrie Wilkerson, known as the Barefoot Executive, once told me that when she posts updates for her subscribers or when she tweets she talks about cities and general areas where she is traveling and what she's working on but never mentions her time schedule or the hotels where she overnights. She often talks about her husband and children and lesson-learning situations in their lives, but she never mentions their names, where the children go to school, or what their sports teams are called. That depth of transparency wouldn't be necessary for her subscribers to feel they know her. Carrie's authenticity combined with the regularity of her artfully chosen level of transparency has achieved for her an intimacy with her market that results, according to her, in almost no return of product. She is so engaging with her market that by the time someone buys one of her programs they feel they are buying from a trusted friend.

IT'S NOT TOUCHY FEELY, BUT . . .

Before I get more practical about employing transparency in your endeavors I'll conclude these thoughts with an idea that may challenge your readiness to see transparency as a significant element of marketing. So please bear with me. The whole point of the challenge toward transparency in our personal and commercial relationships, I believe, is to encourage what is essentially the *laying on of hands* to borrow a religious phrase. That's what is basically going on in social media when mutual good will gets a little personal.

Think about a time you had a private face-to-face conversation with a mere acquaintance such as a neighbor or co-worker and the exchange turned for a moment to reveal something needing your encouragement. However you responded, if you're a good person you likely felt something in your gut that made you want to touch their shoulder and tell them it's okay or relay a similar personal story to show they aren't alone. If you have many Facebook friends and watch your News Feed daily you'll often witness people touching others this way electronically. It's just as welcome, when needed, as the real thing.

Not meaning to get too syrupy about it, I want to emphasize that applying just the right amount of transparency in situations from personal blogs to customer service replies should draw people into your world or the world you are representing. It doesn't have to be heavy and deep. It just needs to be genuine, spontaneous, and human to leave a mark on another person. In a one-on-one customer service exchange it might just be a closing remark like, "Hey, ya'll be safe on the road to Disney World, John, and if you think of it call back when you return and ask for me. I'd like to know how it's changed since I was there as a kid." Though unlikely, if John does indeed call back in a month to tell you all about it, you will not remember him to your great embarrassment (not to mention the damage to your company's authentic identity) if when you said that to John you weren't being authentic. To say something like that you have to genuinely want to talk to John about Disney World because you *did* go there as a child and may want to take your own kids soon. Otherwise, it's just a game and a ruse that will eventually bear the fruit it deserves.

If deception, however well-meaning, is in the mix and widespread in your company interactions with people, human instincts will eventually kick in and some of the public will sense deceptiveness in your company, about which some will post comments. The rule about transparency that even supersedes keeping it appropriate is, *keep it real.*

GUIDELINES FOR TRANSPARENCY

Once you have worked past questions about an appropriate level of transparency there is really only one thing to perfect as you put your policy of transparency into practice on social media:

Let your human side draw people in. You want to make people glad to be part of your sphere. "People will go to any length to find and connect with others."[75] So connect with them. If an opportunity arises in a tweet exchange or on the customer service line to share something personal, genuine, and relevant then share it briefly. Be careful not to abuse time and be sure to keep it relevant. Maybe something funny about your day applies or the wisecrack your wife volleyed at you yesterday. Maybe a complaining customer drifts off to a totally unrelated concern but one you just happen to share. Don't see it as wasting your time and cutting into your call quota. Seize the moment and maybe win a friend for your company.

Customer relations productivity is more than time management. If you're a customer service officer, train your people to think in terms of *relationships* and trust that as they learn to work that way efficiently, the policy will result in operational savings overall. Thinking long-term applies here too, but here's why it pays in the long run: *when all else is as it should be, transparency builds strong customer relations.* In fact, done right, transparency is the super food of relationships. The outgrowth of a strong relationship of any kind is commitment. If your customers feel connected to your company and your product or service through their relationships with you and your people, their innate desire to stay connected will give them a sense of commitment to you. That will translate over time into better customer retention and less customer follow-up management.

Committed customers can benefit the marketing and sales budget as well. We all know it costs less to keep existing customers than it does to create new ones. Management consultants Frederick Reichheld and Earl Sasser, set the rule of thumb back in 1990, in a Harvard Business Review paper saying: "Companies can boost profits by almost 100 percent by retaining just five percent more of their customers, whether you are a Big Six accounting firm, Microsoft, or Olga's Blintz and Borscht Parlor."[76]

Throughout this book what we've been talking about is recovery of the human element in human transactions. During what's often labeled the "Mad Men era" (let's just say the 1950s to about the late 70s) it was common for sales and advertising folks to say with gusto, "Nothing happens until someone sells something." However technically accurate that statement may be, I confess I really don't like it and I don't think it inspires much empathy in real people. What we should be saying now is, "Great things happen when real people connect transparently and trade well." We don't have to be afraid to show our human side or fear the time lost on a moment of connection with our customers. That's like regretting the cost of fertilizing your tomato plants or checking for leaf cutters. If you want great tomatoes you don't mind the investment. If you want to benefit from the opportunities of our digital environment you need to learn the art of transparency with your market. It is an art. And with help from many fine colleagues who also work in the digital space every day, we're making it a fine art.

RESPOND

FREQUENTLY

& THOROUGHLY

Years ago I was on a flight with a layover at Dallas/Fort Worth Airport and had to change planes between two distant terminals. I didn't realize how distant until it was pointless to back track and take the train. On the long walk I decided to poke fun a little and post a tweet that read, *Forgot how big DFW airport is. I guess I won't need my evening run tonight.* It wasn't much more than a minute later that I got a response on Twitter from someone in the DFW business office saying, *We like to keep our customers healthy (smiley face). Next time you can use train [such and such] between terminals A and B.* I hadn't even mentioned to which terminal I was walking but I know what to do next time. That long walk wasn't so very stressful but the unexpected and quick personal attention gave my day a big boost. I didn't feel so anonymous anymore. Someone in the DFW office reached out and connected with me to make me feel welcome and acknowledged.

I now tell that story to crowds to which I speak about the power of pursuing customer relations through social media. The room full of surprised looks and nods I always get says it all. Everyone who's ever felt the anxiety of traveling can instantly understand my experience that day. Even if that were the only time DFW did something like that they've gained a lot of good will with all the people to whom I've told the story as well as everyone who was following me on Twitter that day. But the speed of their reply tweet tells me that DFW is aware of how valuable that little tool is. Imagine it happening hundreds of times a day and all the resulting recommendation stories told.

TIMING IS EVERYTHING

A 2014 report found that 42% of Facebook users expect a response from a brand within 60 minutes. Thirty-two percent expect a response within a half hour! The demand is high, but the payoff is also extraordinary:

- **56%** of consumers who interact with a brand feel a stronger connection with the brand.

- **50%** of consumers are more likely to buy from a brand they can contact on social media.

- **71%** of consumers who receive a quick and effective response are more likely to recommend that brand to others.

THE CONVERSATION BEGINS WHEN YOU SHARE IT

Commenting on the results of a DEI Worldwide survey , Marian Salzman of Euro RSCG Worldwide PR said, "[Marketers] have to realize the conversation is social... In other words, the conversation doesn't take place in the beginning like when you and I have it, but when you share it with the person you talk to next."

"We need to recognize that we need to get the story out there and participate in the storytelling, but that the story is going to be replayed again and again like a game of telephone," he says in *AdWeek.*[79]

Personal and genuinely caring customer relations are so powerful because for far too long this has been unexpected. As the consumer economy grew over the decades so did companies' customer relations difficulties and expenses. Then came the automated customer service line and now consumers are hacking their way through a menu labyrinth just to hear a live human voice. But to be fair, companies in the mass marketing era were dependent on the customer to call back or engage somehow. There was no other way to know about and respond to problems. And when a problem was dealt with, little benefit to the company was realized except the possibility of retaining one customer. With the exception of that hopeful result, after-sale customer service was the sucking chest wound of a company's accounting ledger.

But now service, retail, and media companies can be personal and approach customers, viewers, and listeners right where they are in view of the public and show they care. Companies now have the tools to do what they could never efficiently do before. They can pick up on specific individual experiences and engage people directly in moments that have self-replicating potential. Nothing is more powerful in marketing than an unexpected gesture of connecting and caring right when a customer needs it. All it took for DFW was the right keywords or hashtags in a Twitter search to pick up my tweet so they could find me in need of a little encouragement. And if a company rep does it genuinely and authentically, not using commercial-sounding talk or anything backhandedly promotional, he will gain a customer that will be his to lose. Customer relations also have to be maintained because all human relationships, even commercial ones, are based on good will and trust. The question always in the back of the customer's mind for companies they want to trust is: *Are you still there?* But once a company's core identity is established as genuine and truly customer service oriented, it takes very little using social media tools to draw people in.

Nothing is more **POWERFUL**

in marketing than an

UNEXPECTED GESTURE

of **CONNECTING** *and* **CARING**

right when a customer

NEEDS IT.

Another story, which has become somewhat famous, is about Zappos, the online direct seller of shoes and bags: A woman wanted to return a pair of her husband's boots within the allowed one year return policy, which is an amazingly generous policy in itself, explaining that her husband had recently died in a car crash. The customer service rep promptly refunded the woman's money and sent her the prepaid return shipping label. After the call he decided, without even checking with his supervisor, to also send the woman a bouquet of sympathy flowers from the company. This is the kind of customer relations enthusiasm that propelled Zappos to the stratosphere in sales, made it Fortune's 23rd best place to work within ten years, and prompted a billion dollar buyout by Amazon. When the enthusiasm is spontaneous, authentic, and timely the payoff is a snowball effect of spreading consumer recommendations that millions of dollars spent on Super Bowl commercials and other media ads will never match.

GUIDELINES FOR RESPONSIVENESS IN THE ATTENTION ECONOMY

Above all else be attentive. Strive to reach the place where you can be aware of any and all mention of your company and products online. There are some very snappy applications such as Google alerts and Twitter search that that you can plug in and use to monitor online traffic. Such plug-ins don't interfere with anyone's privacy but merely notify you of a tweet or other open platform review that may be relevant to you and that you may want to respond to. This is a simple function that is added to your overall social media infrastructure and is attended to by customer service personnel. Beyond that, you need to keep a close eye on your own website's ratings and reviews page and respond quickly to all posts, but especially negative ones.

A music video posted on YouTube called "United Breaks Guitars" went viral because United didn't attend to a passenger's claim and complaint after baggage handlers were seen tossing his guitar case resulting in damage to his Taylor guitar. The point isn't whether United was truly responsible for the damage but that United didn't attend to a legitimate complaint. The damage to United's customer relations will cost more in the long run than a proper investigation and resolution of the matter. It wasn't very smart to brush off a talented songwriter. In contrast, Southwest Airlines may or may not be a better airline overall but judging from its integration with social media, it is much more in sync with consumer behavior in the digital space.

Keep it simple and real. When you respond to comments or reviews, be human and not canned. Don't be wordy or try to impress anyone. The social media world is level ground so don't posture or imply a higher vantage point. Recognize that your customers have experience with your product and that their experience makes their perspective legitimate. When you can tell that they may be mistaken on something, try to address it with a question rather than a statement. Statements can sound dismissive and accusing but then so can questions if you don't watch your tone. Another way is to talk about what your company has experienced rather than your company's expertise. Bring people into your experience instead of putting them in their place. When text isn't enough to work out a problem it may be best to invite the customer to call your phone extension and talk it out. Then, instead of saying, "Well, did you read the directions?" try, "Hhmmm! I'm not sure why that happened. Maybe we should start at the beginning. Do you have the directions handy?"

Remember that trolls and haters feed off of fear. When it's not an irritated customer with a legitimate concern but someone who just wants to hurt you, it may be a case when it's best not to pet a growling dog. If (1) the attack is posted someplace like ripoffreport.com and not on your company's review page and (2) it's a clearly irrational attack with no useful opening for helpful dialog, then you best just let it lie. Replying will strengthen the search position of the hostile post and may only sound like "sic 'em" to an angry dog.

If the negative post is on your company review site or perhaps the anger is mixed with workable information about what went wrong for the customer, don't get emotional or counteractive. Be cool, professional and, in this case, impersonal. If you choose not to respond to comments like, "I hope a tornado hits your building," your silence will not evoke suspicion from by-standing readers. But if you do reply, be as unemotional as a computer. Something like, "It would be wrong of us to assume our service/product is right for everyone and it seems likely we aren't right for you. We will continue to work at increasing the number of people we can serve well." When the user responds again even more harshly (as a troll will because you didn't take the first bait) he's just drawing you into the ring with him. Don't oblige him. Don't respond. Your first reply was enough.

Make your Customer Relations Management (CRM) system user-friendly. This has to do with companies that maintain a separate customer service workforce. It is most important to enable your reps with user-friendly systems to help them be more responsive. It's doubtful your customer relations overall can be any friendlier than the management system employed to interact with them. To attract new customers and retain existing ones, the whole purpose of CRM, your system needs to function effectively. Goes without saying, right? Not so fast! There are two ways you can try to improve customer relations management effectiveness, and by now you should be able to tell which one falls in line with the spirit of our current digital environment.

Here's a simple illustration... Call center managers will tell reps if they smile while talking to prospects and customers they will sound friendlier on the phone, even though the customer can't see them. Managers will monitor calls and watch the reps to be sure they are smiling and following script. But what if a rep doesn't feel like smiling for a work-related or personal reason? The two ways to handle that are to pressure them to smile anyway or make it easier for them to smile if possible. The first way considers the rep a component of the system that just needs to adapt and come up to speed. The second way considers the rep a person that perhaps could use some attention to discuss a problem.

So on the larger scale of CRM you can pressure your system users to adapt and work more effectively with complex groups of data and an interface that is difficult to understand and navigate or you can train users well to use an intuitively designed system that is an extension of how humans think. That's user-friendliness and it frees up your users to interact with customers more responsively.

I realize this is an over-simplification of the task. How you accomplish this will best involve the users as well as management and your system designers. But my intention is to get across a concept of cooperating with human inertia for the greater benefit instead of using counter-force to steer against inertia. Shape your tools so they fit a human hand. CRM tools and protocols can become very complex as a company grows. The more attention you give to keeping them user-friendly the more your workflows benefit.

EMBRACE THE RATINGS & REVIEWS ENVIRONMENT

I'll grab your attention right off the bat by saying that ratings and reviews can be the best entry door for social media marketing without having to first rework your company's entire culture. This opinion is shared by Lance Loveday of Closed Loop Marketing who saw early on that the conventional advertising model wasn't going to work on social media platforms. The reason is that, for users, social media is about interaction with other users, not attention to buying opportunities.

A 2015 survey found this is *especially* true with the under-30 demographics. Seventy-five percent of these Facebook users are likely to share a video that's been shared on a friend or family member's wall. However, only 46% are likely to share a post by a brand that has been shared multiple times in their network. (Keyword there: *multiple*.) So, while a personal post by a friend or family member is likely to be shared, brands have to work for *multiple impressions,* and even then... it's significantly less likely to be shared.[80]

Social media exists for the users – not for brands. (Of course, it likely benefits your brand to have strategically placed promoted posts, Facebook ads, etc., as these products do impact sales.) Because users hold so much sway on social media, the concept of ratings and reviews can be the scariest aspect of social for marketers. It feels safer to have a well-designed advertisement do all the speaking for the company and avoid as much negative feedback as possible. Many marketing companies have added Internet defense to their services for clients. There are also a few companies that specialize in helping companies minimize online comment damage – especially from trolls and haters.

Besides utilizing defenders, one of the best ways to mount a defense is to be well-positioned offensively beforehand. In September 2015, Volkswagen found themselves at the nexus of one of the automotive industry's biggest crises to date. The car manufacturer was found to have falsified emission levels in several of their models. Worse – the computer sensors in the cars were deliberately calibrated to display EPA-friendly figures during testing. The elaborate lie had snowballed over several years. Over 8.5 million vehicles were recalled in Europe alone. (Investigations and rulings are still going on at the time of publishing this book, but it's possible as many as 11 million vehicles may be affected worldwide.)[81]

When the news broke, Volkswagen was nimble enough to act quickly on their Facebook page. In a post dated September 25[82], Volkswagen came clean with their Page Fans about the situation, writing a lengthy (for Facebook) apology that included statements such as this: "We sincerely and deeply regret that we have abused your trust. We will take care of all your concerns quickest possible."

Volkswagen had done the hard work up front of building trust and loyalty on social media. So, when a crisis came along, the company didn't have to start from scratch. Instead, they came clean, apologized, and refocused their digital strategy to include language about "transparency, openness, and diligence."[83] In addition to the digital work Volkswagen did in advance, the brand is very human and relatable. Years of Volkswagen brand messaging, like those we discussed in chapter two, have established the name as an ally and asset for businesses and consumers.

FEAR OF CHANGE GETS US NOWHERE

The focus of attention should be on the achievable destination not on the stone bruises we might get along the path. What companies need to achieve more of are consumers who become brand advocates. BzzAgent reports that, among their clients' customers, brand advocates are 85% more likely to recommend their preferred product than Web users overall. [84] That is a desirable percentage in any time but in the social media age it can mean exponential growth. Brand advocates duplicate themselves many times more rapidly through social media than ever before.

When it comes to ratings and reviews, the proof is in the pudding. Consumers are increasingly turning to peer reviews before making purchasing decisions... and those reviews are directly tied to sales. One massive study that analyzed **57 million reviews** and **35 billion product page views** discovered that even moderate increases in the number of reviews a product has increases the return on investment:

• 1-8 reviews increases conversion rate

• 8+ reviews start noticeably affecting organic search traffic

• 100+ reviews allow for product insights

Reviews are invaluable in our digital culture, where information-ownership has been transposed from brands to consumers. A study of influencer marketing tells us that **92%** of consumers trust recommendations from other people (even someone they don't know) over branded content. **Seventy percent** of consumers reported online customer reviews as the second-most trusted source.

WHEN THERE'S A BEEF

And now we come to the straw boogeymen of social media. You really can relax about online complaints and negative reviews. Negative feedback is not the river Styx you may fear and your complaining customer isn't the boatman. Don Zeidler, Director of Marketing at Burpee Garden Products, explains that negative reviews actually help establish legitimacy to a company's review pages. They show an unfiltered honesty and confidence on the part of the company. "When customers see a mix of different ratings they are more apt to trust the review process. Negative reviews help customers affirm they've vetted all concerns before making a purchase decision. John Squire of Coremetrics remarks, "We're always surprised by how much negative reviews help drive sales." Ian Greenleigh at Bazaarvoice could be considered the horse's mouth when it comes to the effectiveness of even negative ratings and reviews. He points to five proven advantages they provide over no reviews at all:[87]

• *Negative reviews add to a company's reputation of authenticity and credibility especially if answered wisely.* For the time being consumers still expect companies to make every effort to present a clean, wrinkle-free face. When they don't and leave negative reviews up for all to see it is still a little bit of a surprise. The confidence and honesty it shows is impressive enough to elicit a closer look.

• *Products and services with more reviews, even if they're negative, get more clicks than products with fewer or no reviews.* So any reviews are better than none, especially, again, if a company knows how to respond to negative reviews authentically and transparently with a commitment to improved quality control and customer service.

• *Negative reviews alert companies to product flaws that can then be addressed.* This actually creates an opportunity to publically display a process of product improvement. We've already seen how this also creates a sense of ownership among consumers who contribute negative reviews and then witness results in the form of product or service improvement. The loyalty momentum for a customer that is brought back into the fold this way can be even greater than for a customer that is satisfied from the start.

SOCIAL MEDIA

IS ABOUT

INTERACTION

WITH OTHER USERS,

NOT ATTENTION

TO BUYING

OPPORTUNITIES.

• Negative reviews provide a more realistic view of the product to customers. They return this product less often, because they know what they're getting and aren't surprised by shortcomings. What a customer could be surprised by, however, is discovering that the negative reviews weren't justified in his case. This will make a positive rebuttal review very likely, which will decrease the impact of the negative reviews.

• Companies might think if they don't invite reviews, they simply won't have to deal with them. Instead, they end up having to address these reviews outside of their "home turf," in the social Web where they have far less control and influence. Letting the conversations take place on company websites makes more sense because conversations are more easily tracked, complaints are easier to address and results are far more instantaneous. I will add that handling complaints or problems close to home will also minimize the search results ranking of negative and malicious posts on third party review sites like ripoffreport.com and improve the rankings of your site with added content. This is one of the simple strategies of online *reputation management* employed by ORM companies.

GUIDELINES FOR EMBRACING
A RATINGS AND REVIEWS MINDSET

Consult with application pros. There are so many different ways to approach implementing a review system for your products or services; it pays to have experienced help in choosing a design and strategy most appropriate for your products and business model. Meet with people who can help with this. Be armed with a list of good questions generated from your own survey of companies in your industry and other companies that have implemented rating or review functions on their websites. Companies like Bazaarvoice, Power Reviews, my company BuzzPlant, and others can partner with you to determine the best formatting and integration with your existing web infrastructure.

Grow a thick skin. Moderate what appears on your review pages, but state openly that only posts with offensive or abusive language (especially if directed at specific persons) will be subject to removal. Stick to this as a general policy but don't use it as an excuse to remove otherwise relevant posts by a customer who just needs to vent. Take negative reviews on the chin and give a human response (i.e. not scripted or glib) that shows willingness to work things out with the customer. Contrary to looking weak, handling emotional customers in an agreeable, patient manner actually makes you look very strong if you show you respect the customer but also respect yourself. A very good book, if a little dated, dealing with constructive and destructive patterns of verbal exchange is *The Gentle Art of Verbal Self-Defense* by Suzette Haden Elgin available from Amazon. If you've ever wondered how to stop a verbal attack in its tracks and make it harmless and even constructive with one brief, artful reply, Ms. Elgin shows how.

List with friendly review sites and avoid the troll pits. There are product specific and general review sites where you can list your company and invite reviews of current promotions and products. If you haven't listed your brand on general review sites you may have already been listed on some by site users. In most cases you can reclaim any listing not posted by you to make sure information is correct. But care needs to be taken when posting replies on review sites to determine if it will result in a net benefit. The culture of the site is usually detectable and many worthwhile sites are well known.

Most reviews on sites like *Yelp.com*, *Citysearch.com*, and *Tripadvisor.com* are positive or at least well intentioned because these sites encourage genuinely useful information from users. This means they are less attractive to malicious reviews, such as those by a disgruntled former employee, because they won't be as likely to generate a string of "me too" follow-up posts as will sites like ripoffreport.com. Even though many reviews tend to be valuable there as well, online reputation management (ORM) companies like Reputation Advocate discourage companies from responding to reviews on ripoffreport.com or on similar broad topic review sites. The result of responding even very courteously to a negative review (especially a hate review) on sites where trolls are known to haunt will likely be to improve the position of the negative review in search results connected with the mentioned brand, thus creating a more visible opportunity for other trolls to chime in.

Savvy social media marketing professionals are tuned in to these hazards and can navigate through them while helping you engage consumers beyond your in-house Web interactions. Attracting trolls and net negatives, of course, is a small risk whenever and wherever you engage social media users about your brand. But you can limit the risk and keep the balance tipped to your benefit by limiting your engagement on review sites to those that serve well-defined markets. Examples are *Yelp* and *City Search* that offer information and review platforms about businesses local to the user.

Trip Advisor focuses on transportation, hotels, and other travel services. Sites that cater to certain demographics are another category. AARP, AMAC, and other organizations for seniors, for instance, have message boards and interactive blogs on their websites with specific topics significant to their memberships.

It's vital that you utilize Google alerts and Yahoo alerts using keywords and brand names to alert you to posts anywhere on the Internet that mention anything important to your marketing efforts. Then you can decide if engaging will have a net benefit or poses a questionable risk.

SOLOPRENEUR CASE STUDY: JOEL COMM

Joel Comm, author, speaker, consultant, and entrepreneur is a jack of all trades. He's a *New York Times* best-selling author; he has spoken at TED Talks and IBM events; and, since 1995, he has pioneered a number of profitable websites, software, and products. Joel is a *doer*. He makes things happen. While you could chalk up his success to intelligence, hard work, and being at the right place at the right time, there's another key ingredient...

Joel, like so many other solopreneurs who have enjoyed success on this side of the dot-com bubble, *knows how to communicate in a human way*. That's it. Joel is human as they come in the communications department. It resonates through all of his content and the way he interacts with his audience online.

Many of Joel's posts on social media reveal his desire for being human and *real* online – not just another voice adding to the noise. A few of my favorite Joel quotes include:

- "Who's willing to stand up and say, 'I'm a human being and this is all I got?'"

- "People love an inch deep and a mile wide, but why not be a person of substance?"

- "Passive Aggressive: Posting something you want to say to someone on your Facebook wall without saying that person's name."

You can see Joel's character through these statements, posted as memes to Facebook and Instagram or Tweets to his 85,000 followers. Joel cares deeply about restoring his audience. His purpose is giving, sharing, and creating genuine connection and community. But who better to tell you about Joel... than Joel? Here's a conversation with my good friend, Joel Comm.

JOEL COMM IN HIS OWN WORDS

Finally Human: In a recent talk at IBM, which was very entertaining, you were discussing how high-tech/low-tech doesn't really matter. What matters is making your message memorable. How do you think that a business can make a really memorable message in the content-saturated world that we live in, where we're just getting barraged all the time?

Joel: I think ultimately it's about good storytelling, right? Everything goes back to the story; stories have been handed down through generations, and whatever the medium is, whether it's the written word, spoken word, or however we're doing it now, whether it's live video, recorded video, through a blog, through any of the different channels of dissemination - billboards - everything tells a story, and you've got to be willing to tell a story that is so interesting and compelling that your target market will retell it for you at no cost.

Finally Human: Yeah, the retelling is a huge part of it.

Joel: It's what we call viral marketing, really. That's really what viral marketing is. You don't create viral marketing, you create compelling stories, and then people decide if it's viral or not.

Finally Human: Right. And you've been doing a lot of stuff on Periscope[88] lately, which we see as being a much more human platform with its live-streaming ability, its lack of editing function... do you have any comments on what you like about that platform?

Joel: Yeah, I've been doing live streaming since 2008, so it's nothing new for me. Now that we have it on mobile, it's so easy to pick up a device and either in the moment share what you're experiencing or to actually have a strategy and plan a show. So, examples of both...

A few days ago I woke up around seven in the morning to the sound of what I thought was the trash man – *BEEP, BEEP, RRRR* – you know, all these sounds. And I'm kind of dozing off, and I wake up again, and I still hear the sounds. I'm thinking, "That can't still be the trash man." So, I hop out of bed, look out my window, and I've known for months that the house next to me was scheduled for teardown. The owners were going to build something new; they were tearing down the house. I grabbed my phone, went outside, and did this Periscope of the claw tearing down this home that's been there since the 50s, and it was amazing. I had tons of people watching because it was in the moment and it was cool as heck. Ok, so that's the spontaneous type of broadcast that I love.

Then, we have the planned show. I've got a program that I do now called the Top 5 Scopes.[89] [Periscope] allows me to do it whenever I have time and whenever I have the inspiration – no more than once a day – of my top five whatever-it-is, whether it's top five social media tips, or personal development, or thoughts about travel, or why I like going to a certain place or doing a certain thing or enjoying a certain kind of food. It's all *me*. So, rather than being put into a box format, it can be whatever I'm inspired to do that day. Yesterday it was "Top 5 Reasons I'm Giving Snapchat a Try." [The show] allows me to be on Periscope, broadcast to my audience, and keep it brief. I spend the first few minutes welcoming people, getting them to share, telling me where they're from, and then I go into the official show, which lasts usually 10 to 12 minutes and I'm done. Then I download – you said there was no editing in Periscope, and that's true, but for repurposing, there is – I download the scope to my phone, I chop off all the welcome stuff at the beginning, and I put some music and titles on it, export the video, put it on YouTube, upload it to Facebook, and write a blog entry and embed the YouTube video there. So, I'm taking that Periscope content, and I'm making it live forever. Repurposing!

Finally Human: A lot of people – they just don't get it – would say, "Joel, why are you doing your top five lists on where to get a hamburger in Arizona or something, when you don't have anything to do with hamburgers? You're a speaker, you're an entrepreneur." How would you explain or justify that behavior to those people who just don't get the social space?

Joel: Well, number one, I don't have to justify anything to anybody. Number two, I'm not going to do a scope about top five hamburgers in Arizona if I'm not interested in the top five hamburgers in Arizona. I'm only going to cover and talk about something that I actually want to talk about. That's why I chose that template or framework for my show - because it's about "what Joel thinks." It's not about what other people think. It's about what I think. That's the way I treat all of social media. I don't launch different pages for each one of my brands. I am the brand. So, people learn that, "Well, whatever *Joel* is doing is what I'm interested in..." then it doesn't matter what I'm talking because they know that I'm going to be passionate and interested in what I'm talking about, and they're trusting that the content they're going to get comes from a real place, and that's what brings us around to social: that social has to be real.

The facade needs to come down, and we need to connect on social like real people. And there are so many that are pretending to be something that they're not. That's way too much work for me; it's way easier to just be myself with all my flaws, foibles, and imperfections, than it is to put up this facade. That's why I don't wear a suit and tie anymore when I speak. I'm more comfortable with jeans and a t-shirt – maybe a sports jacket – because that's who I really am. And I think people connect with that.

Finally Human: Throughout the majority of the last 100 years in marketing and advertising, brands are always asking things of customers. They're demanding things. They're pushing the sale, sometimes using underhanded techniques... there's a lot of broken trust between consumers and the *you've got to be*

WILLING *to* **TELL A**

STORY *that is so*

INTERESTING

&

COMPELLING

that your **TARGET**

MARKET *will retell*

it for you

at **NO COST.**

businesses selling to them. How do you see social media, or the current digital space, as being an opportunity for fixing that trust?

Joel: Well, first of all, brands don't have a choice anymore. You know, it used to be that if people felt deceived, they would call and tell a friend that they didn't like how somebody marketed to them. But now, they post it, and *all* their friends see it, and so we have these – for lack of a better word – lynch mobs that come out in full force when somebody is upset about something. And *that* story goes viral.

You know, it's the stupid thing with the Starbucks cup[90], which paints a whole group as complete morons. But the fact is, it's a handful of morons, right? A handful of people that are like, "Bring back Christmas! They took it off the cup!" [As if Starbucks is] somehow indebted to make a certain type of cup for Christmas. But that whole thing went viral, and there was this public backlash and now Starbucks is probably selling more coffee in plain red cups than ever before. So, brands need to be aware of how they're behaving and what backlash could take place. Listen, it wouldn't surprise me if someone at Starbucks said, "Here's what we're going to do. We're going to take snowflakes off of our cup, and then–" I'm not saying they did do this, but I could see it as a brilliant marketing campaign if they had "– and then we're going to have somebody rant against it." They could have planted that whole thing, and what'd they get? A hundred million dollars worth of free advertising out of this thing. It's brilliant! And it wouldn't surprise me if that's how it went down.

Finally Human: Back to broken trust...

Joel: You will be found out! That's it. You will be found out, so just be straight up and real, and if you do screw up, say you're sorry. It's not hard. "Hey, guess what? This Tweet was insensitive. This post had incorrect data. This is what we should have done or said. We're sorry, please forgive us. And it's amazing how many people are incredibly forgiving towards an individual or a brand that is humble.

Finally Human: To what degree do you think that businesses should try to act like actual *people* on social media? Saying you're sorry is a very human thing to do.

Joel: A hundred percent. To a complete degree. In every aspect. I don't see a reason to hide behind your logo in your brand. We are entering into an age where "real" is a currency. Oooh. I like that. Being *real* is the new currency. I'm going to have to photo quote that. I'm writing it down. I'm going to photo quote that when I'm done here. Sometimes I say something, and I'm like, "Wow! Where'd that come from?"

Finally Human: For solopreneurs or really small businesses, where's the line between being authentic, genuine, deeply human, and then crossing over into an overly-personal, unprofessional kind of sharing?

Joel: Well, everybody needs to understand what healthy boundaries are, right? There are different circles of trust that we have. You know, you've got your inner-circle which is those people that you're most intimate with, that you share some of the deeper struggles of your life while you're going through it: it could be a spouse, a significant other, it could be your parents, could be your best friend at work, it could be your mentor or your boss... but there's appropriate levels, right? And then you go out from there, and now you've got your wider circle of friends and your associates. And you go out from there and you've got your strangers, the general public.

Discernment is something that is sorely lacking in human beings. There's not a manual: *Share this, not that! Tell this person this, but don't tell this person that!* Discernment is learned through experience, and it comes through wisdom. Some of the smartest people I know are the most foolish. They don't have wisdom; there's a big difference between knowledge and wisdom. So, I think discernment comes from wisdom, and brands need to make sure that the people that are communicating their message are wise people. Those that are interfacing with the public, they don't just need to be smart. I would rather they be wise, rather than be chockfull of knowledge. And, so, it's a case-by-case basis.

I don't know that I've really ever got in trouble for sharing much. I know my personal boundaries, and what I will share and what I won't. And I know where my life is public and what part of it is private, and I don't cross that line. Let me just give you an example. About six weeks ago I went offline. I told everybody, "I'm unplugging for two-and-a-half weeks."[91] It was a personal sabbatical where I was leaving social media completely. I was not handling any of my work emails – my VA was going to handle it and would only forward me what was essential – and I was going to just go take care of myself, and then I would be back. Well, when I got back, people wanted to know, "Where did you go? What did you do? Who were you with?" I didn't tell them. It was *mine*. It was *my* business where I went. It was *my* business whom I was with. It was *my* business *why* I went, what I learned there, the 1200 pictures that I took. They're mine. And they weren't to share. Everything doesn't need to be a matter of public record, and there's something about that that people really respected. They weren't like, "Aw, come on, tell us."

They were like, "Wow! That's really cool. Not only did you unplug, but you kept that part of your life to yourself." And I think it inspires others to maybe do the same, go, "You know what, maybe a little unplugging and just breathing fresh air isn't such a bad idea."

Finally Human: And having the wisdom to know when to do it and how much about it you can share.

Joel: Yeah. Amazingly, sometimes I even get it right!

If you enjoyed Joel's interview, visit joelcomm.com, and say hello!

MID-SIZED

BUSINESS

CASE STUDY:

RUBY

RECEPTIONISTS

Ruby Receptionists are living proof that a business-to-business service doesn't have to use boring communications. I have been repeatedly impressed by how this Portland-based "real, live virtual receptionist" service markets itself. The company, which was founded in 2003 by Jill Nelson, has won numerous awards for its employee culture and beliefs. Ruby frequently appears on lists of "Best Places to Work" in Oregon and throughout the U.S.

Not only is Ruby a great place to work and an invaluable asset for its clients, the company is *crushing it* on social media! Ruby's communication all stems from its clear, actionable Core Values. I'd like to share an excerpt from each of their five Core Values with you:

> • **Foster Happiness:** "We're a happy bunch, and we like to make others happy. Every day, we wage a war on impersonal service and stressed out workdays."

> • **Practice WOWism:** "We don't do fine—we hit it out of the park. Nothing gives us a bigger kick than impressing our clients and team members. More than impressing, really — surprising, delighting, *WOWing.*"

> • **Create Community:** "Our clients don't view us as faceless operators, but part of their team, and we view them as part of ours. When our clients win, we win."

> • **Innovate:** "'That's the way it's always been done' is not a reason to keep doing what we're doing. We are not confined to 'standard operating procedures.' If it's not working for us, we'll change on a dime."

> • **Grow:** "We aren't afraid to make mistakes; we're risk-takers at heart and each decision makes us wiser. Change inspires us, and learning is a life-long passion."

Maybe you feel like you *know* Ruby after reading their Core Values? I know I came away feeling like I had received some genuine, *real* insight into what this business stands for.

Now, you might be a skeptic, and think, *Sure, Core Values are nice, but who really pays attention to them besides management?* Well, Ruby pays attention to them – the whole company does, according to their site: "Our Core Values [...] are not something you hear about on your first day and file away in a drawer. We use them to make all of our decisions, big and small. Every Ruby knows them by heart (go ahead, quiz 'em!) [...]"[92]

It's hard to take any old website copy at face value. Of course, they're going to put their best foot forward, right? So, let's turn to social and see how Ruby Receptionists isn't just paying lip service on their website; they're *living* out those values through social media.

Ruby maintains an active presence on Facebook, Twitter, Instagram, and LinkedIn. On the first three platforms, they use the catchy handle @callruby across the board – great way of sharing just a little bit about what they do, while keeping the name short and consistent. That one move already shows us that Ruby is thinking clearly and with *purpose* in their approach to the digital space.

Ruby on Facebook

Facebook appears to be Ruby's bread and butter.[93] It's where the brand is showing the most personality – and they certainly have a *lot* of personality, thoroughly dispelling any preconceived notions you may have about B2B companies being dry or boring in their communications.

Ruby uses a variety of post types, primarily (1) links to interesting articles, (2) photos-quotes about work ethic, (3) links to Ruby blog posts, and (4) "Fashion Friday" photos from around the office that tell the company's story. While Ruby does a good job with types 1, 2 and 3, they do an **incredible** job with type 4. Perhaps more so than any mid-sized company I've seen before, Ruby is actively sharing company culture through Facebook photos. And – even better – it all looks 100% genuine. It isn't hassled, "put-on," or over-produced; it's just real, which makes it incredibly restorative in a sea of fake social media posts.

Check out their page to see some examples of their "Fashion Fridays." You'll quickly see that these aren't just photo albums of employees in their best dress. Instead, they're funny, creative, offbeat themed collections that encompass everything from Dr. Seuss to Pixar to Friday the 13th. Employees really go all out on these Fridays. Take a look at their Fashion Friday: Puns album[93] to see the lengths these employees will go in getting creative.

As we've already discussed in this book, on-the-job silliness and cutesy plays like Fashion Friday won't work for every company on social. But for Ruby, whose entire brand image is built around themes like happiness,

NOT HASSLED, "PUT-ON," OR
OVER-PRODUCED; IT'S

just real

WHICH MAKES IT INCREDIBLY
RESTORATIVE IN A SEA OF
FAKE SOCIAL MEDIA POSTS.

community, and innovation, these post types are homeruns. The content comes across as *human* because Ruby does one thing really well: **Ruby successfully marries company culture and social media.**

Plain and simple, that's it. Ruby's company culture is fully displayed on social media, and Ruby's social media *only* displays its company culture. Therein lies Ruby's success. Here is what it all boils down to:

1. **Decide** who you are.

2. **Be** who you are.

3. **Tell** people who you are through social media.

4. Only use social media to tell the story of who you are. **Don't dilute** it with messaging that doesn't reinforce your brand.

Before we move on, let me give you one more example of how Ruby's Facebook strategy embraces their identity – but this time, without any of the lightheartedness that's so close to the brand's core. If you remember back to Ruby's Core Values, one of those values is "Innovate." Part of Ruby's innovation includes a "Green Team" that volunteers to find ways the company can reduce waste. Ruby shared a story about the Green Team's activities with this friendly Facebook status and two pictures illustrating the new changes:

"Did you know Ruby has a 'Green Team?' These employees volunteer to find ways to reduce Ruby's waste. Recently, one of their members saved 29 binders worth of printed material by moving meeting documents online AND eliminated our wooden coffee stirrer waste with a reusable spoon system. Way to go!"

Practically any company could run a post like this on Facebook (as long as it were true to the company's ideals and values). It's simple; it doesn't require any high-production value... what's not to love? It's a feel-good piece of micro-content that reinforces Ruby's "innovate" identity. What a great example of how simple it is to create a meaningful piece of genuine content.

Ruby on Twitter

First and foremost, Ruby gets the gold for not having the one terrible habit that 90% of brands on Twitter have. Can you guess what it is? (Ok, there are a lot of bad habits...)

...Ruby doesn't use Twitter as a second Facebook.

It's frustrating when a Facebook page you love simply uses Twitter as another means of pumping out the exact same content. Where's the value in that? Fortunately, that is *not* the case with Ruby. This is the first thing that sets them apart from their competition. Whoever is running the social media at this company has recognized the platform's inherent differences and *respected* those differences by publishing unique content to each.

Ruby's Twitter feed is split roughly 50/50 between their own content and other users' content. Not bad. The company has done a good job acknowledging that Twitter is a *social* platform and not a channel for broadcasting. A lot of Ruby's Twitter content is just so-so ("three tips for such-and-such," "5 business mistakes to avoid," "how to focus better," etc.) – you know the type.

However, Ruby will throw out a genuine, human-sounding Tweet like this one[96] every few days, in which they express gratitude to a client. While Ruby's Twitter content and community engagement is average, they do get points for posting different content than what appears on their Facebook page and for showing effort. Perhaps, in time, we'll see their use of this platform mature to a stage where it rivals the quality of their Facebook account.

Ruby on Instagram

Ruby does an excellent job showing us what a business-to-business organization can look like on Instagram. If you thought this platform was only for your sunset pictures and fine-dining spreads, then look at how Ruby's using it. While some of the content we see here also appears on Facebook, the majority of it is unique to Instagram. Props to Ruby for this achievement; they make the experience of following @CallRuby and 'liking' their Facebook page worthwhile for their audience: two unique stories, two unique perspectives.

Let's look at a few of the Instagram posts that make @CallRuby worth following...

Special Delivery

In this post[97], we see a Ruby Receptionist smiling and holding a huge stack of seven or more boxes with the word "delivery" marked on the front. The caption says, "What's more fun than WOWing a client with a special gift after creating a wonderful connection?" This is a great post for a number of reasons: it's an interesting photo, it's intriguing (*what's in the boxes?*), and it reinforces one of Ruby's five Core Values: "Practicing WOWism." Well done! This post was published on a business Instagram account, but it could have just as easily been posted by an office employee, which means Ruby Receptionists is hitting a homerun in the "being human" department! Oh, and one other thing I love about this post – it contains a perfect mix of hashtags: #PracticingWOWism (that one's Ruby-specific), #CoreValue (used by companies and organizations around the globe), and #ThatsALotOfBoxes (playful, fun... Ruby!).

Ray of Sunshine

Here's another playful and valuable piece of micro-content. In this post[98], @CallRuby celebrates National Customer Service Week (this is post one of three) with a fun shot of an employee holding a sign that says, "I adore being a ray of sunshine on someone's cloudy day" (her answer to the question, "What do you love about serving clients?" The look on her face makes us believe her, too! "Foster Happiness" is the first of Ruby's five Core Values, and this snapshot hits the mark.

If you work in the business-to-business sector and want to learn how to use Instagram in a meaningful, human, way, follow @CallRuby. I expect we will see more good posts from them on this platform!

Ruby: A Human Name for a Human Brand

It makes sense that Ruby Receptionists has an actual person's *name* embedded in their company name, doesn't it? This brand is human, through-

and-through. I love seeing how they reject the false "brand v. human" dichotomy we discussed earlier in this book. They are completely in-tune with how brands can – and *should* – act "human" in all of their communications. Along the same lines, Ruby knows that "being human" is complicated. People have different sides – different moods – and Ruby has learned how to play up those different sides across its social media platforms.

It's been fun seeing how Ruby actively *restores* its employees, clients, and audience on social media. Can you imagine a world where *every* business had communications that were this genuine and engaging? (I wouldn't be writing this book!) As we've discussed earlier, this type of genuine communication is becoming increasingly common as more brands wake up to the realities of the Attention Economy. Ruby's ahead of the curve, and I think they will do an excellent job leading in this area as more brands follow suit.

BIG BUSINESS CASE STUDY: WAZE

Waze is **big** (50 million users is the latest statistic, and it's certainly dated), **well-funded** (a Google product since 2013, and **cool** (Silicon Valley, crowd-sourced, social, etc.). So, if we're going to take a deep dive into a "big" brand that's being *human* in its communications, then let's go *BIG*, right?

If you aren't familiar with Waze, it's an app that bills itself as, "the world's largest community-based traffic and navigation app." Just by having the app on your phone, you contribute real-time data to the Waze network. Waze also allows users to input specific data that can help the community. If there's a road closure or an accident, report it (all hands-free, of course) so that other users will know to avoid it.

Waze, by nature, is a restorative product. It's actively fixing something that's been a broken and frustrating part of daily life: *the map*. Whether you're using an old road atlas, a web-printed route, or a less-intelligent smartphone app, chances are, your map – and therefore your knowledge of your surroundings – isn't nearly as robust as it could be if you were using Waze.

Waze is also a very human product. It appeals to that spark in each of us that wants to do the right thing and help out our community. Gamification is another core part of Waze's identity that resonates with our human nature.

Just because a product is "human," we can't assume that its communication strategy will also be "human." But in Waze's case... that human element does bubble out into the company's behavior on social media. Let's look at how Waze is creating its own content and using Facebook and Twitter to build genuine human connection with its audience.

Waze & Content Creation

Essential to Waze's voice is... well, *everyone else's voice*. It's a community-sourced platform, and it only works as well as its users. It's fun to see how Waze has twisted this essential truth into good marketing by developing seasonal, limited-time-only navigation voices. Arnold Schwarzenegger lent his voice in promotion of *Terminator Genisys*, C-3PO's voice made an appearance prior to *Star Wars: The Force Awakens*, and other celebrities like Stephen Colbert and Colonel Sanders have even shown up on Waze. This is the kind of creativity and execution that brands with deep pockets and a wide pool of resources should be considering. The marketing stunts tend to work well by piggybacking on personalities that their audience already *loves*.

By creating a personalized experience, Waze offers users something more than mere product placement. Instead, Waze uses these characters to give back to movie buffs. By securing these characters, the company is actively restoring the consumer's broken understanding of a free product/service's potential. The message we get is: Just because Waze is free, doesn't mean it should be minimal.

Remember those three questions we asked in chapter four?

1. Is my brand's online voice a genuine expression of our company culture?

2. Am I creating content that's valuable/useful/helpful/interesting to my audience?

3. Am I being restorative?

Waze knocks them out of the park with its recurring celebrity-partnership play:

1. Absolutely. Waze is all about community and fun. So, shaking things up with a special, surprise navigator voice makes sense.

2. Useful, helpful? Maybe not. But valuable and interesting? Certainly! What *Star Wars* fan, driving around in holiday traffic, wouldn't appreciate a little humor and optimism from C-3P0? Waze is going above and beyond to deliver a remarkable product to the user.

3. Are the company's actions "restorative?" I would argue they are. Waze is upending the noting of what a GPS navigator voice "should" be with these special features. Instead of limiting users to a dry, formal, and overly-articulate voice, Waze is giving users a *friend*, someone the user already likes, knows, and trusts.

Waze gets five stars for content creation. Let's look at how they share those stories...

Waze on Facebook

Like many larger brands on Facebook, Waze only posts content once every few days. The logic behind this content strategy is usually along the lines of, "Facebook will only share so much of our content with our Page Fans, so let's make our content more rare (and therefore more likely to be displayed) by only posting when it *really* matters." Maybe this approach works; maybe it doesn't. With the volatility of Facebook's algorithm changes, it's not that important of a question, as what's true now about how Facebook works may not necessarily be true by the time you read this book.[99]

Regardless, from a *human-touch* viewpoint, this Facebook publishing strategy works well for Waze. The occasional posts are one way of telling Page Fans, "We think everything we share with you is important. We aren't trying to fill a content calendar, and we won't put out anything that's just mediocre." In that sense, Waze is the kind of brand that you want to hang out with. They're friendly, real, and human. They aren't going to waste your time either. In our content-saturated world, that's *definitely* a restorative characteristic.

Waze on Twitter

While Waze's lack of regular content is fine on Facebook, a similar approach on Twitter is a little *too* lackadaisical... Twitter is a platform where brands can be constantly involved in the pop-culture, tech-culture, political-culture, pick-your-culture conversation. And for a brand as big as Waze, choosing *not* to be active in those conversation is a little foolish.

Before you get the impression Waze's Twitter account is all bad, let me show you the good things they're doing. Waze has a fervent commitment to following up with Twitter users who ask questions, air grievances, and express general confusion about how the platform works. This is surprisingly uncommon with many large companies on Twitter, so props to Waze for at least participating in the "Waze conversations" on Twitter if nothing else.

There is one drawback though. Unfortunately, Waze speaks in waves. There will be nothing but static silence surrounding @Waze for days, and then – suddenly! – several dozen or even hundred replies to a backlog of frustrated users. This scenario is indicative of a common problem many large companies face on social media. On the one hand, they know they they *should* be social and sometimes they *want* to be social, but they haven't dedicated the resources to do it right. Reading between the lines here, I would wage that whoever runs @Waze probably wears many hats and only hops onto Twitter when he or she has a few free moments.

Just because

a **PRODUCT** *is*

HUMAN

we can't assume

that its

COMMUNICATION

STRATEGY

will also be

HUMAN.

Compare Waze's Twitter behavior to an even larger mobile-based app like Spotify, and you'll see the difference between sporadic, hurried responses and dedicated, well-thought-out responses. I don't have to dig deep at all to turn up example after example of Spotify responding to "@ mentions" with clever playlist titles that complete their Tweet. This is a typical Spotify exchange:[100]

User says, "Love how @Spotify tells me good morning every day."
Spotify says, "Hey Alex! We just want you to [*link to a playlist called "Wake Up Smiling"*] :)"

That's clever, right? It's human. It's real. Spotify cranks out that kind of micro-content all day long. Perhaps, as Waze matures, we'll see more of this clever and conversational content develop on its Twitter profile.

Waze Everywhere Else...

Waze excels on Facebook and Twitter, so it's really a shame that they only put forth mediocre effort (that's being generous) on two other major platforms: Instagram and Google+. At the time of writing, it's been 78 weeks since Waze posted to Instagram and 16 weeks since posting to Google+. With such dismal activity levels, Waze would probably be better off shutting down its accounts on those platforms and pointing users over to Facebook and Twitter, where the real Waze conversations are happening. (Of course, being a Google product, their hands may be tied when it comes to the Google+ account.)

When it comes to social, Waze is a mixed bag – which is exactly why I like them as a case study. They do some things *really well*, other things pretty poorly, and – like all of us – tend to land somewhere in the middle on a lot of areas. Waze as a case study shows us a few things:

> 1. As I said at the beginning of this case study, Waze is big, well-funded, and cool. But those three things don't automatically add up to a dynamic human presence on social, do they? No matter how big your company is or how much money you have, being human takes work. Waze has put in the effort in some departments (like content creation), but not in others (like real-time Twitter response).

2. A string of off days *can be* okay on Facebook when 100% of the content you *do* post is quality. It just doesn't work the same on Twitter. You're either there for the conversation, or you're not.

3. Inactive profiles should just be deleted. In the case of Google+, Waze should abandon and concentrate on the platforms where its users congregate. In the case of Instagram, while its users are definitely there, it appears that Waze doesn't have time to be there, which is a shame, considering how many of its users are probably on Instagram. If making that time just isn't an option right now, a formal hiatus from Instagram may be worth considering.

There are small and mid-sized brands that could run circles around Waze's communications. Then again, there are much bigger brands that would give an arm and a leg to have the social acuity and execution Waze does possess in the digital space. If nothing else, I hope these three case studies have shown you that size isn't the most important factor. **Being human** can happen at *any* size and with *any* budget. It just takes hard work and practice.

THE FUTURE BELONGS TO THE HUMAN BRANDS

We have seen the evolution of brand behavior gradually shift over the last 100 years from mass-market directives to personal, value-adding communications. With the rise of social media, niche marketing, and the Attention Economy, this trend has accelerated. In the coming years, we will see a greater number of brands adapt more "human" voices and personable styles of communication. But the revolution is still in its infancy.

Revolutionary Che Guevara said, "The revolution is not an apple that falls when it is ripe. You have to make it fall." In other words, change can be slow in coming about. If you want to see a change in how our culture communicates, start with yourself. After reading through many examples in this book, you know you won't be alone, but you may be the first in your industry, network, or market to start using a restorative, human, and truly *personal* style of communication.

The brands that will win in the future are the ones that grab their share in the Attention Economy now before "human-like" behavior becomes increasingly common. Remember our example about the lawn care business in chapter four? Years ago, your lawn care company could be the top lawn care brand on Facebook simply by being there and posting good content. Today, there are already hundreds of brands with good content on Facebook, and the local lawn care company that wants to rise to the top must put in a lot more effort than simply showing up and cranking out good content. They have to cultivate a **genuine voice**, create **valuable content**, and act **restoratively**. Brands who embrace these efforts will win by *leading* – by being first-responders to changes in the environment. These behaviors are the new frontier of the communications landscape.

As more businesses discover success by practicing the three core behaviors mentioned above, the Attention Economy will tighten once more (i.e. user-attention will be captured by the brands who know how to act like humans, thereby shrinking the supply of 'attention' for brands that are late to the game). Currently, "being human" is something of a novelty in brand communications. It isn't very common and it certainly isn't *expected* by consumers. However, it's only a matter of time before "being human" is the new baseline for successful brand communications.

START TODAY.

Perhaps, as you've been reading this book, you've already taken the first few steps in experimenting with your brand's voice and behaviors online.

Or, maybe you're the type who wants to finish the book, reflect, and wait. I urge you...

Don't wait.

You will not solidify your brand's voice and communications strategy right out of the gate. These behaviors are learned over time through trial and error. If you wait for your brand's voice to be perfect before starting, you will never start. So, start now, because...

The future belongs to the *humans*: the brands who understand their audience, respect their audience, and deliver **valuable content** with a **genuine voice.** Don't wait for that "moment of inspiration. Just start now.

A NOTE ON EMERGING TECHNOLOGIES

People are slow to accept new technologies. In the Introduction of this book, we briefly discussed how new forms of communication – beginning with written language itself – were initially met with resistance. The printing press, the telephone, email... *emoji*... all of these forms of communication have been scoffed at, suppressed, and written off as valid forms of communication by various groups throughout their introduction to mainstream culture. Of course, we now know they are valid and – more so – effective forms of communication. (Yes, even emoji. Six billion are sent around the world *per* day,[101] and 84 percent of females and 75 percent of males believe "emojis express their feelings more accurately than words."[102]) Communication styles change. If you want to effectively spread a message, riding the crest of the wave should become habit.

The marketplace is about to shift in some big ways with the Internet of Things (IoT) and proximity-based technology. These two sectors (and the concurrent rise of Big Data) *will* present major challenges for brands that are not already acting in a genuine, "human" way, which is why they are worth a brief discussion before concluding this book. There are two reasons I see these tech sectors as being some of the most important to watch in the coming years:

1. Some of the largest projected growth figures are in these two industries.

2. These industries make **many** consumers **very** uncomfortable.

COMMUNICATION STYLES CHANGE. *If you want to* EFFECTIVELY SPREAD A MESSAGE, **RIDING THE CREST OF THE WAVE** *should become* HABIT.

Whether these technologies **pull** you or **push** you, they will change your company. For some companies, these technologies present new venture opportunities worth considering (a "pull"). Other companies will see their current operations model, marketing plan, supply chain, etc. totally disrupted by the IoT and proximity-based tech (a "push"). Whether the future *presents opportunity* or *necessitates change* for your company, one thing is certain: brands who know how to communicate in a human, relatable way will have a much easier time breaking into these emergent industries while growing an audience that trusts them.

If these terms are not familiar to you, here's a brief introduction...

The Internet of Things: Estimates from Cisco, Intel, and the IDC say there could be between 26 billion and 212 billion devices connected to the IoT by 2020.[103] "The Internet of Things" refers to an Internet of non-traditional items that connect to the Internet and other devices. Common household IoT products include lamps that can be turned on and off remotely, thermostats that learn your routine, and showerheads that can play your music library. In the ideal future world, your car will tell your thermostat that you're coming home early from work and that it should go ahead and turn up the air-conditioning so your home is nice and comfortable when you arrive.

While many consumers would agree that the benefits of IoT technology are great, there are plenty of concerns about data security and a "Big Brother" dystopia. Even amongst those who *desire* the technology, there is concern about how it could be used.

Proximity-Based Technology (NFC/RFID/iBeacon/Eddystone): Hardware developers are locked in competition to develop proximity-based tech that's widely adapted by both brands and consumers. While the details vary between Apple's iBeacon, Google's Eddystone, and other Bluetooth low energy devices, they all offer similar functionality. The idea is that retailers, hospitality businesses, and consumer good manufacturers (among many other sectors) can embed a tiny chip in their storefronts or products to broadcast messages to consumers with Bluetooth devices. No app or opt-in is necessary on the part of the consumer, which is one reason why this technology has had so much difficultly getting off the ground. (As we've learned... consumers don't like being *shouted* at or *marketed to*. The very concept of blasting out a message for anyone walking by is very much out-of-line with the way our culture thinks.)

Obviously, there is huge potential for these technologies. Proximity tech allows brands to reach customers with special offers and targeted information. It also allows consumers to improve their own lives. For example, you could set up an iBeacon at your desk that would detect your presence (via your smartwatch or smartphone) and send a message to your wife to let her know you arrived safely to work.

Again, concerns about these products are very legitimate. Proximity-based technology will make many people feel as though their privacy is being taken away. Even if consumers *like* the benefits, many will take an even stronger *disliking* to the drawbacks.

'HUMAN' BRANDS WILL HELP SOLVE THESE ISSUES.

The rise of Big Data, as briefly summarized above, is one of the biggest issues that our culture will wrestle with in the coming years. Brands that can understand the hesitancy of users who aren't confident and excited about getting on board with this technology have a shot at winning big in this digital environment.

As the technology enters the mainstream, people will have questions and concerns. By meeting those people where they are and talking through their questions in a **genuine**, **value-adding**, and **restorative** way, brands have a huge opportunity.

WHAT IF I'M NOT DOING ANYTHING WITH EMERGING TECH?

Don't sweat it. These emerging tech examples (which, by the way, probably will affect all businesses in the same way that mobile has impacted all businesses over the last five years) are just one example of future applications for the strategies we've already learned in this book. Whether you manage a Silicon Valley startup accelerator or run a purely brick-and-mortar, on-site retail operation, the same philosophy still applies:

People everywhere are in need of validation. You have the opportunity to restore individuals and to restore the means that you use to communicate with them.

WILL YOU JOIN ME?

It's time for our humanity to enter our communications. Let's redeem our communications, our industries, our local and global economies, our users, our audiences, our fans. All indicators show the leading brands moving this direction. It *will* happen. The question is: will you tag along once the shift in thinking is complete? Or will you join me now in leading a revolution in how we approach communications?

NOTES

[1] http://www.psmag.com/books-and-culture/is-facebook-stunting-your-childs-growth-40577

[2] https://www.psychologytoday.com/blog/reading-between-the-head-lines/201307/smartphone-addiction

[3] http://www.huffingtonpost.com/2013/05/03/internet-porn-stats_n_3187682.html

[4] http://www.itv.com/news/wales/2015-03-31/one-in-ten-12-13-year-olds-worried-they-are-addicted-to-porn/

[5] http://www.forbes.com/sites/moneybuilder/2015/01/13/the-big-data-breaches-of-2014/

[6] https://www.psychologytoday.com/blog/cultural-evolution/201008/write-or-not-write-or-what-plato-didnt-know

[7] http://scottsauls.com/2014/09/24/mean-missional-living/

[8] http://money.cnn.com/gallery/real_estate/2014/03/27/fastest-growing-cities/7.html

[9] http://buzzplant.com/is-influencer-marketing-the-next-golden-ticket-info-graphic/

[10] http://www.ted.com/talks/sherry_turkle_alone_together/tran-script?language=en

[11] https://www.youtube.com/watch?v=5HbYScltf1c

[12] http://www.sciencedaily.com/releases/2015/01/150111195734.htm

[13] http://www.baylor.edu/mediacommunications/news.php?action=sto-ry&story=145864

[14] http://www.huffingtonpost.com/2013/05/03/internet-porn-stats_n_3187682.html

[15] http://www.huffingtonpost.com/elwood-d-watson/pornography-addiction-amo_b_5963460.html

[16] http://www.prweb.com/releases/2013/2/prweb10382447.htm

[17] http://www.charismanews.com/opinion/watchman-on-the-wall/41611-pornography-addiction-a-growing-problem-among-women

[18] http://www.ted.com/talks/zimchallenge?language=en

[19] http://www.ted.com/talks/jane_mcgonigal_gaming_can_make_a_better_world

[20] http://mashable.com/2014/06/05/edward-snowden-revelations/

[21] http://www.pewinternet.org/2014/11/12/public-privacy-perceptions/

[22] http://mobile.nytimes.com/2015/02/05/style/why-google-glass-broke.html

[23] http://www.npr.org/2014/02/25/282359480/social-media-researcher-gets-how-teenagers-use-the-internet

[24] https://books.google.com/books?id=4o1oBAAAQBAJ&lpg=PT140&ots=soX5qlvo6p&dq=%22when%20you%20show%20deep%20empathy%22&pg=PT140#v=onepage&q&f=false

[25] http://buzzplant.com/100-years-of-brand-storytelling-an-infographic/

[26] http://lunarmobiscuit.com/selling-the-first-telephone/

[27] http://faculty.atu.edu/cbrucker/Engl5383/Marketing.htm

[28] ibid

[29] http://adage.com/article/adage-encyclopedia/history-1920s/98699/

[30] ibid

[31] https://youtu.be/ABcckOTVqao

[32] http://articles.chicagotribune.com/1987-07-12/features/8702210177_1_tv-ad-cigarette-ads-sara-lee

[33] http://adage.com/article/special-report-the-advertising-century/ad-age-advertising-century-top-100-campaigns/140918/

[34] http://www.nytimes.com/2010/07/06/business/media/06adco.html?_r=0

[35] http://sethgodin.typepad.com/seths_blog/2007/12/big-ideas-meatb.html

[36] https://youtu.be/2JnYcuRW_qo

[37] http://sethgodin.typepad.com/seths_blog/2008/01/permission-mark.html

[38] http://www.eater.com/2014/8/5/6177213/yelp-turns-10-from-startup-to-online-review-dominance

[39] http://buzzplant.com/new-science-behind-trust-recommendations-social-media-infographic/

[40] http://www.forbes.com/sites/kylewong/2014/09/10/the-explosive-growth-of-influencer-marketing-and-what-it-means-for-you/

[41] http://www.profitadvisors.com/ogilvy.shtml

[42] http://buzzplant.com/is-influencer-marketing-the-next-golden-ticket-infographic/

[43] http://buzzplant.com/new-science-behind-trust-recommendations-social-media-infographic/

[44] https://hbr.org/2011/06/the-only-thing-that-really-mat.html

[45] http://www.apa.org/news/press/releases/2012/03/well-being.aspx

[46] https://youtu.be/ol19tt3VWhQ

[47] https://www.facebook.com/lowes

[48] https://www.facebook.com/lowes/app_1387359808211576; also https://www.lowesrantorrave.com/

[49] http://industry.shortyawards.com/nominee/7th_annual/op1/new-vines

[50] https://vine.co/Lowes

[51] http://charlesandhudson.com/lowes-fix-in-six-vines/

⁵² http://passionpassport.com/

⁵³ http://www.entrepreneur.com/article/241670

⁵⁴ https://www.youtube.com/watch?v=PjGuh2Fbic4

⁵⁵ https://www.tacobell.com/404

⁵⁶ https://www.facebook.com/tacobell/posts/10153581239824697

⁵⁷ https://www.facebook.com/tacobell/posts/10153309231414697

⁵⁸ http://www.fastcompany.com/3041640/most-innovative-compa-nies-2015/the-worlds-top-10-most-innovative-companies-of-2015-in-advert

⁵⁹ https://www.youtube.com/channel/UC-8aMX2uL1Mt8MgojmNvn4w

⁶⁰ https://instagram.com/p/8YYIsTDYUx/

⁶¹ https://www.facebook.com/gary/videos/10153612348278350/

⁶² https://www.facebook.com/gary/videos/10153606991928350/

⁶³ http://sethgodin.typepad.com/seths_blog/2011/12/getting-seri-ous-about-the-attention-economy.html

⁶⁴ http://sethgodin.typepad.com/seths_blog/2011/07/paying-atten-tion-to-the-attention-economy.html

⁶⁵ https://beme.com/

⁶⁶ http://www.wired.com/2015/07/beme-authenticity-boring/

⁶⁷ https://today.yougov.com/news/2014/04/08/truth-advertising-50-dont-trust-what-they-see-read/

⁶⁸ http://www.nielsen.com/us/en/insights/news/2013/under-the-influ-ence-consumer-trust-in-advertising.html

⁶⁹ Scott Brinker, Chief Marketing Technologist, 3 takeaways on advertising and trust from Nielsen, http://www.chiefmartec.com/2011/09/insights-on-advertising-and-trust-from-nielsen.html

⁷⁰ Jamie Monberg, Authenticity is Kink Because Branding Bores Everyone, Co.Design blog, Feb. 25, 2001 (http://www.fastcodesign.com/1663269/au-thenticity-is-king-because-branding-bores-everyone).

[71] Rohit Bhargava, *Personality Not Included: Why Companies Lose Their Authenticity and How Great Brands Get it Back*, 4.

[72] http://www.socialmediatoday.com/content/social-media-transparency-how-realistic-it

[73] http://www.socialmediatoday.com/content/65-terrific-social-media-infographics

[74] http://www.socialmediatoday.com/content/social-media-transparency-how-realistic-it

[75] Eric Whitacre, TED Talks, March 2011, (http://www.ted.com/talks/eric_whitacre_a_virtual_choir_2_000_voices_strong.html).

[76] Fredrick Reichneld and Earl Sasser, *Zero Defections: Quality Comes to Services*, Harvard Business Review, Sept. 1990 (http://hbr.org/1990/09/zero-defections-quality-comes-to-services/ar/1).

[77] http://buzzplant.com/brand-savvy-social-first-responder-infographic/

[78] *The Impact of Social Media on Purchasing Behavior*, DEI Worldwide commissioned white paper, (http://www.deiworldwide.com/index.html).

[79] Marian Salzman quoted by Stacy Straczynski, *Social Media Users Really Are More Social*, Adweek.com, Nov. 20, 2009.

[80] http://buzzplant.com/everything-to-know-about-your-audiences-social-media-habits/

[81] http://www.consumerreports.org/cro/cars/guide-to-the-volkswagen-dieselgate-emissions-recall-

[82] https://www.facebook.com/volkswagen/posts/1158617350834314

[83] https://www.facebook.com/volkswagen/photos/a.179087015454024.48452.126633520699374/1169305869765462/

[84] BzzAgent, *Characteristics of Brand Advocates*, (www.bzzagent.com).

[85] http://buzzplant.com/proven-product-reviews-generate-sales-infographic/

[86] http://buzzplant.com/is-influencer-marketing-the-next-golden-ticket-infographic/

[87] *From interview with Mack Collier, (http://www.mackcollier.com/setting-the-record-straight-on-online-reviews-an-interview-with-bazaarvoices-ian-greenleigh/).*

[88] *https://www.periscope.tv/*

[89] *http://joelcomm.com/the-top-5-scope-for-those-who-love-lists.html*

[90] *http://www.cbc.ca/news/trending/starbucks-red-holiday-cups-controversy-jokes-and-backlash-1.3312326*

[91] *http://joelcomm.com/18-days-without-you.html*

[92] *http://www.callruby.com/our-story.html*

[93] *https://www.facebook.com/callruby*

[94] *https://www.facebook.com/media/set/?set=a.1143925462304255.1073741884.107944562569022&type=3*

[95] *https://www.facebook.com/callruby/photos/a.111292032234275.12918.107944562569022/1156407111056090/?type=3&permPage=1*

[96] *https://twitter.com/callruby/status/668929552538841088*

[97] *https://www.instagram.com/p/-AOMuKltSe/*

[98] *https://www.instagram.com/p/8gu7U9FteA/*

[99] *On the other end of the spectrum, there are large Facebook pages like Gary Vaynerchuk's – 475k+ fans and counting – that publish three to five times per day and continue to get impressive engagement. So, really, there's no definitive right or wrong answer on which approach is better.*

[100] *https://twitter.com/alexcbafile/status/672387273623781376*

[101] *http://digiday.com/brands/digiday-guide-things-emoji/*

[102] *http://buzzplant.com/the-emoji-infographic-stats-to-back-up-your-obsession/*

[103] *http://www.forbes.com/sites/jacobmorgan/2014/10/30/everything-you-need-to-know-about-the-internet-of-things/*

ABOUT

BOB HUTCHINS

Bob Hutchins (Franklin, TN) is the founder/CEO of BuzzPlant (www.buzzplant.com), a 15+ year old digital marketing agency. Since 2001, Bob has strategically guided online campaigns for countless movie/books/music-releases and events, including Mel Gibson's *The Passion of the Christ*, *The Chronicles of Narnia*, *Soul Surfer*, and *Blue Like Jazz*. His client/partner roster includes Time-Life, Sony Pictures, General Motors, Twentieth Century Fox, INO Records, Disney, Warner Brothers, Thomas Nelson Publishers and Zondervan.

As a marketing expert, author, and cultural interpreter, Bob is uniquely positioned to help brands understand how to communicate digitally in a style that is human and relatable.

Bob is a frequent blog contributor at Social Media Today, Business2Community, and Digital Journal, and occasionally teaches Social Media Marketing to MBA students at Belmont University (Nashville, TN). He has been featured on Fox News, MSNBC, in The New York Times, Wall Street Journal, INC Magazine, Fortune Magazine, MarketingVOX, American City Business Journals, Dallas Morning News, and on various television/radio media outlets.

HOW DOES
MARKETING AND
ADVERTISING IMPACT
THE HUMAN SPIRIT
IN A NOISY,
CONTENT-SATURATED
WORLD?

BETTER QUESTION: HOW SHOULD IT?

As brands, businesses, and organizations, how do we turn something as uninteresting or even at times offensive as "advertising" into an enriching experience for our audience? How can we use our digital tools and social environment to restore people–leaving them better than we found them?

Finally Human explores these questions and offers solutions through proven strategies and thoughtful case studies. With the tools in this book, you will learn how to enhance the humanity of those around you, while also communicating your brand's message in a powerful and irresistible way that resonates with your audience.